SARAZEN

SARAZEN

The Story of a Golfing Legend and His Epic Moment

David Sowell

ROWMAN & LITTLEFIELD
Lanham • Boulder • New York • London

Published by Rowman & Littlefield
A wholly owned subsidiary of The Rowman & Littlefield Publishing Group, Inc.
4501 Forbes Boulevard, Suite 200, Lanham, Maryland 20706
www.rowman.com

Unit A, Whitacre Mews, 26-34 Stannary Street, London SE11 4AB

British Library Cataloguing in Publication Information Available

Library of Congress Cataloging-in-Publication Data

Names: Sowell, David, 1948- author.
Title: Sarazen : the story of a golfing legend and his epic moment / David Sowell.
Description: Lanham : ROWMAN & LITTLEFIELD, [2017] | Includes bibliographical references
    and index.
Identifiers: LCCN 2016035126 (print) | LCCN 2016039833 (ebook) | ISBN 9781442265554 (cloth :
            | ISBN 9781538130964 (pbk) | ISBN 9781442265561 (electronic)
Subjects: LCSH: Sarazen, Gene. | Golfers—United States—Biography. | Golf—United States—
    History—20th century.
Classification: LCC GV964.S3 W69 2017 (print) | LCC GV964.S3 (ebook) | DDC 796.352 [B] —
    dc23 LC record available at https://lccn.loc.gov/2016035126

For Domenic and Roseann
An inspiring couple

CONTENTS

I

SETTING THE STAGE

That day in 1935 when Bobby Jones putted out to complete his final round, you could feel the sense of disappointment in the crowd at the 18th green at Augusta National. Like the year before during its inaugural edition, it appeared that Jones's tournament was again not going to meet the expectations generated by its tremendous hype.

It was the first Sunday in April, but the weather was more like the first Sunday in February. An hour after Jones finished his round, Craig Wood, the leader by three strokes, was exiting the 18th green and making his way to the clubhouse. A few minutes earlier Jones, who had been tending to his duties as the tournament's host in and around the clubhouse, decided to go back out on the course and follow the few remaining groups back to the home hole.

Of the handful of players still out on the course, none appeared to stand a chance of catching Wood. As Jones made his way back on to the course, many of the patrons began to make their way to the parking lot. Little did they know that in just a few minutes, the most famous shot in golf history would be struck.

The Great Depression had begun on Black Friday, back in October 1929. For the game of golf, it didn't start until Black Monday, November 17, 1930, when Jones, the greatest player the game had ever known, decided at age 28 to announce his retirement from competitive golf. At that moment, golf joined the rest of the country in a grim stall. The game languished there until February 1934, when it received a huge jolt of adrenaline. Albeit for just one tournament, Jones was coming out of retirement to play competitively again.

For most of the previous four years, Jones had been busy planning and building his dream course in Augusta. To showcase his creation, he was hosting the Augusta National Invitational Golf Tournament. Soon after announcing the plans for the early spring event, Jones decided he was going to make a one-time exception to his retirement and announced that he was not only going to host the tournament, but play in it as well.

For the next six weeks, the sports pages and the golf world were abuzz with anticipation. On the eve of the tournament, although he had not played a competitive round in almost four years, oddsmakers made him the favorite at six to one.

By his own admission, Jones had played more golf in retirement than he ever had during the years he played competitively. But for those who had put their hopes, and in some cases cash, on the second coming of Bobby Jones, his return to competition did not live up to their expectations. Jones's play, although respectable, was not the world-beater brand of his glory days. He finished 10 strokes behind the winner, Horton Smith, in 13th place.

In the run-up to this second staging of the Augusta National Invitational Tournament in 1935, an event some had been calling the "The Masters" from its outset, Jones again announced he would come out of retirement to play in the tournament. The pre-tournament hype surrounding his entry was every bit as rousing as it had been the year before. And once again, he was listed as the favorite by bookmakers. Unfortunately Jones's performance once again failed to meet expectations. In fact, it did not even match his showing the year before. When he tapped in for par at the 18th hole to complete his final round, he was 15 strokes behind the leader.

Had Jones delayed his departure from the clubhouse area by just a minute, he would have missed being in that very small number that witnessed the most epic shot in golf history. As he reached the top of a mound along the fairway of the par-five 15th hole, he paused. To his left, some fifty yards away, he could see the pairing of Walter Hagen and Gene Sarazen and their caddies. Sarazen, some 235 yards from the pin, was beginning to address his second shot; Hagen and his caddie were standing about 20 yards to Sarazen's left. A few moments later, Sarazen fired off his shot with a 4-wood. Years later Jones gave this account of that moment: "His swing into the ball was so perfect and so free, you knew immediately it was going to be a gorgeous shot."

As Jones was working his way back out onto the back nine that fateful Sunday at Augusta, Grantland Rice, the country's most noted sportswriter, was in the clubhouse with most of the rest of the press corps, enthralled with what was setting up to be one of the feel-good stories of the year—Craig Wood winning Jones's tournament. Wood had suffered a heartbreaking setback the previous year in the first Augusta National Invitational, losing to Horton Smith by a stroke. What made this moment even sweeter was that this day was Wood and his wife's first wedding anniversary. Wanting the best pictures for this feel-good story, the press corps goaded the happy couple into posing for a photograph with the winner's check.

Rice, no doubt, had a pretty good outline already mapped out in his head on how he would describe Wood's victory to the millions of readers who would read his nationally syndicated column the next day. Many today consider Rice's writing more than a little syrupy. But for his time, he was at the top of the sportswriters' leaderboard. His most-quoted lines were from his poem "Alumnus Football": "For when the One Great Scorer comes, To mark against your name, He writes—not that you won or lost—But how you played the Game." And he was also known for nicknaming the great backfield of the 1924 Notre Dame Fighting Irish football team the "Four Horsemen" of Notre Dame in his account of their contest against Army in New York City's Polo Grounds. Using a biblical reference to the Four Horsemen of the Apocalypse, he wrote:

> Outlined against a blue-gray October sky the Four Horsemen rode again. In dramatic lore they are known as famine, pestilence, destruction and death. These are only aliases. Their real names are: Stuhldreher, Miller, Crowley and Layden. They formed the crest of the South Bend cyclone before which another fighting Army team was swept over the precipice at the Polo Grounds this afternoon as 55,000 spectators peered down upon the bewildering panorama spread out upon the green plain below.

Whatever thoughts Rice was formulating for his Craig Wood story were in a few minutes going to be abandoned when word reached the Augusta National clubhouse that there was a commotion from the direction of the 15th green.

In describing the cause of this commotion to his readers the following day, Rice borrowed a phrase from the first stanza of Ralph Waldo Emerson's poem, "Concord Hymn," written almost a century earlier:

> By the rude bridge that arched the flood,
> Their flag to April's breeze unfurled,
> Here once the embattled farmers stood,
> And fired the shot heard round the world

Emerson penned the poem in 1837 for a July 4th celebration in Concord, Massachusetts, that commemorated the firing in Concord of what was thought to be the first shot of the American Revolutionary War—a shot many believe established Concord as the spiritual center of the American nation.

Rice chose to use the last six words of the first stanza, "the shot heard round the world," to brand Sarazen's remarkable feat. Although the sound of this crisply struck 4-wood did not match the report of the musket fired at Concord, its impact did create another type of spiritual center for the nation in Augusta, Georgia—this one for the game of golf.

From 1895 to 1910, the first 16 United States Open Championships (U.S. Open) were won by golf professionals who were natives of Great Britain or one of its possessions. All of these champions with the exception of one were golf professionals who had immigrated to America. The one exception was Harry Vardon in 1900. Vardon was the game's first superstar and won the Open while on a tour of the United States sponsored by the A. G. Spalding Sporting Goods Company.

In 1892, a young buyer for Spalding named Julian W. Curtiss was dispatched to England to examine its leather industry as a possible source of supply for footballs. While there, Curtiss ventured onto a course and the golf bug nailed him. He decided that there could possibly be a buck to be made in America with golf, and he purchased a small inventory of golf equipment to sell back in the States.

When Curtiss returned to Spalding's corporate headquarters, his golf purchases became the butt of jokes around the office. His coworkers dubbed his golf inventory "Curtiss's Folly." A. G. Spalding, the company's founder and chief executive officer, was resolved to write off the purchase as a learning experience for his young executive. Curtiss's purchases turned out to be anything but folly, and soon golf products were a major product line for the company. In two years, Spalding was manufacturing its own line of clubs. A year after that, A. G. Spalding had a nine-hole course built on his estate. In 1898 the company began producing golf balls at its Chicopee, Massachusetts, facility. In time golf would make up 40 percent of sales for the company, and Julian Curtiss would become its long-serving president.

In early 1900, Spalding brought Harry Vardon over from England for an extended tour. Vardon played in golf exhibitions up and down the Eastern Seaboard, promoting Spalding's golf equipment. At this point, Vardon had won three of his six British Open titles. In late May, Vardon briefly interrupted his stay in the United States and returned to Great Britain to seek his third consecutive win in the British Open. St. Andrews was the host course. Vardon's quest for three in a row fell short, as he finished in second place behind another British golfing legend, J. H. Taylor, who won the crown for the third time.

A few weeks later, Vardon sailed back to the United States and began touring the Mideast and Midwest. J. H. Taylor followed him over a short time later. Taylor had entered into a partnership with a Pittsburgh golf professional to market clubs in the States, and he had come over to promote the new enterprise. In early October, both Vardon's and Taylor's paths took them to Chicago and the Chicago Country Club to play in the U.S. Open. By the end of the second round, Taylor and Vardon had pulled away from the field, and it was a two-man duel the rest of the way. Taylor slipped slightly in the final round to give Vardon a two-stroke win.

In 1911, Great Britain's streak of dominance finally ended when American-born John McDermott, a 19-year-old former caddie from Philadelphia, won that year's Open. McDermott followed up that historic win with another victory in the 1912 U.S. Open.

The feeling among many in Great Britain's golf community was that McDermott's victories did not portend an emerging standard of the game in the United States that was equal to their own. Occasionally, the States would produce a golfing phenomenon like McDermott but, overall, its players would never be superior to those from Great Britain.

The general consensus was that this line of thought would be substantiated at the upcoming 1913 U.S. Open at The Country Club in Brookline, Massachusetts, just outside Boston, as Harry Vardon was again touring the United States and would be making his second appearance in the championship. Since his last visit in 1900, Harry had won three more

British Open titles. He was being joined on this tour by Ted Ray, another golf standout from Great Britain.

Ray was one of the longest hitters the game had ever produced. Each year from 1906 through 1913, Ray had finished in the top ten in the British Open, recording one eighth-place finish, one sixth, three fifths, a third, one second, and one first.

It came no surprise that at the end of 72 holes at Brookline that Ray and Vardon were in a tie for first place. But in what was a huge surprise, there was a third golfer tied with them, an American, home bred. Whereas Vardon and Ray had traveled some 3500 miles to get to Brookline, this golfer had traveled about 350 feet. He was Frances Ouimet, a 20-year-old former caddie at Brookline who lived in a house across the street from the club.

Twenty-four hours later on a gloomy and damp day, Ouimet defeated the two Brits in a playoff, besting Vardon by five strokes and Ray by six, in what has been described as the coming-of-age moment for American golf.

Great Britain's entry into World War I in August 1914 suspended its golfing rivalry with the United States. It would resume in 1920 at each country's open championship. The British Open was up first, in late June. The American contingent in this event was being led by Walter Hagen, a 27-year-old former caddie from Rochester, New York, who was long on game and hutzpah.

Hagen had made his U.S. Open debut at Brookline in 1913 and finished in a tie for fourth. The following year, he won the Open at the Midlothian Country Club outside of Chicago. In the 1915 and 1916 U.S. Opens, Hagen had a tenth and a seventh place finish respectively. The 1917 and 1918 Opens were cancelled because of World War I. The event was resumed in 1919, and took place at the Brae Burn Country Club in West Newton, Massachusetts, a suburb west of Boston. Given his past U.S. Open performances, Hagen was the favorite going in and he did not disappoint, as he won his second Open title in a playoff.

At the time of his win at Brae Burn, Hagen had the cushiest head golf professional position in the country at the Oakland Hills Country Club outside of Detroit. The club had been founded several years earlier by one of the top executives at Ford Motor Company and an ad agency executive whose main client was Ford. The two men brought in Donald Ross to design its course. Since shortly after his arrival from his native Scotland near the turn of the century, Ross had been setting the standard for golf course design in the U.S. His most noted work was also one of his earliest: Pinehurst No. 2 in Pinehurst, North Carolina. At Oakland Hills, Ross created another masterpiece. Upon its completion, the new club brought in Hagen, considered at the time to be the top professional golfer in the country, to serve as the head professional for Oakland Hills.

Near the end of 1919, the proud members of Oakland Hills threw a big banquet in Hagen's honor for his U.S. Open win at Brae Burn. At the dinner, Hagen received rousing applause as he rose and went to the dais to speak. He gave a gracious and heartfelt speech, thanking the members for their great support. Then, he floored his audience by announcing his resignation as the club's professional.

Up until that point, a golf professional in America was a club pro first and foremost. In the late fall and winter months, he played in tournaments in the West and South. During the spring and summer, except for the majors and a sprinkling of other tournaments, he was on duty at his club. Hagen was giving up his post at Oakland Hills to blaze a new career path. He was going to be the country's first touring professional, devoting his time to competing in tournament play and traveling the country playing exhibition matches.

Almost immediately after announcing his plans, Hagen let it be known that he was circling the British Open on his calendar. From January 1920 until he sailed for Great Britain in May, Hagen hyped with zeal his impending quest for the Open Championship. Hagen's arrival in England received great fanfare in the British press. His swagger and style of play made quite a mark with the Crown's golf fans. In warm-up matches and practice rounds, Hagen appeared to be transitioning well to the style of play required on links courses. Boastful comments attributed to him about his chances in the Open Championship brought the national pride aspect of the event to a nice boil.

The British Open site was along the coast of Sandwich Bay in southern England at the Royal Cinque Ports Golf Club. There were 88 spots available in the Open, and over 160 entrants. Qualifying was broken into two sections, with the top 44 in each section advancing to the Open. Hagen made a strong showing in his qualifier, finishing fourth. But it was a different story when he teed off in the Open Championship. On the first hole, he missed a one-foot putt for par and his game went into a tailspin. He finished in 49th place.

Six weeks later, the 1920 U.S. Open took place. When compared to previous Open sites, its venue, the Inverness Club in Toledo, Ohio, was somewhat off the beaten path. For the first 13 years of its existence, Inverness had been a run-of-the-mill nine-hole club. In 1916, its membership decided it was time to go major league. To that end, they too contracted Donald Ross to design and construct a new 18-hole layout. He plowed under the old course. Over a two-year period, he designed and built a course that, upon completion, was considered another 18-hole Ross masterpiece. In 1919, Inverness hosted the Ohio Open and the success of that event spurred a push for the course to host the U.S. Open. The push developed into an avalanche. By the time U.S. Golf Association (USGA) officials met to vote on a site, all the other contenders had decided to drop out.

Walter Hagen had garnered most of the golfing limelight in the country for the last six years, but there were changes on the horizon. The U.S. Open at Inverness would be the first time that he and two huge future rivals would be in the same field: Bobby Jones and Gene Sarazen. They were both just 18 at the time. Bobby Jones had been earmarked for stardom since he made his debut on the national golf scene at the U.S. Amateur at the age of 14. His picture-perfect swing was something to behold but he did bring some personal baggage to the table—his fiery temper. It often got the best of him during a round, making him prone to club throwing and outbursts of profanity that would peel the bark off of trees.

Gene Sarazen's participation at Inverness was a bit of a reach. In the late fall of 1919, Gene had said farewell to his position as pro shop attendant/club maker/janitor at a Connecticut golf club and struck out for Florida. He was hoping to land an assistant pro position there for the winter season and play in some stops on the fledging pro golf winter tour. But he found Florida flooded with more qualified candidates. To survive, he had to take a job unloading lumber in a railyard. He stayed in a room in a low-rung boarding house and ate as cheaply as he could. Pancakes and sardines were the cornerstones of his diet.

By late winter, Gene had scraped together enough funds to play in a few of the last stops on the winter circuit. In those events, Gene won a meager $75, but playing the winter circuit did lead to his securing an assistant pro position for the coming golf season. The circuit had ended with a tournament in Asheville, North Carolina. At that event, Gene's game impressed a fellow competitor who was the head professional at the Terre Haute Country Club in Terre Haute, Indiana, and he offered Gene a job as his assistant.

Once in Terre Haute that spring and summer, Gene's game made a strong impression on the club's members. Several of them were so impressed they provided the financial support for him to take a shot at playing in his first U.S. Open at Inverness.

Although one man at Inverness would be one of the most well known in the field, his entry in the event was also considered a bit of a reach. His name was Grantland Rice and he would be taking on a dual role at Inverness, covering the event for his readers and teeing it up as well.

When Rice, now 39, was in his late 20s, before his sportswriting career took off, he covered the Southern Open Golf Tournament in his hometown of Nashville, Tennessee, and as a result decided to take up the game. He did so with an ultra-smooth swing and unbridled passion. A few years later in 1911, Rice took a job with an evening newspaper in New York City—the *Evening Mail*. He wrote his stories in the morning and played golf in the afternoon, and was soon ranked among the city's best amateur golfers.

While he had plenty of free time for golf, he devoted little of his workday to covering the sport. His editor believed only stories about baseball, football, and boxing belonged on the sports page. Rice's requests to cover the 1913 U.S. Open at Brookline and the 1914 Open in Chicago were denied.

In early 1915, Rice moved to the *New York Herald Tribune* for twice as much money as he was making at the *Evening Mail*, and his career skyrocketed. *Tribune* readers were more well-heeled and getting into golf in a big way. Rice gave these readers plenty to read about the sport.

Shortly after moving to the *Tribune*, Rice coauthored with U.S. Amateur champion Jerome Travers one of America's first books on golf, titled *The Winning Shot*. When Rice's column went into national syndication, he devoted more of his copy to golf than did any of his peers.

Being part of an event he would be covering was not a new experience for Rice. When he worked for the *Nashville Banner*, he had regularly covered Vanderbilt football games while also serving as one of the games' referees. He had also once covered and played in an amateur golf tournament in Pinehurst. He finished second.

When it was all said and done, there were a record-setting number of entrants, 278. Each one of them shared one thing in common: They would all have to qualify. There were no exemptions, even for Walter Hagen, the defending champion. The schedule for the week called for a 36-hole qualifier that would take place on Tuesday and Wednesday, with the low 68 and ties making the field. The Open would take place on Thursday and Friday, with 36 holes being played each day.

Walter Hagen was likely the last entrant to show up at Inverness. He arrived in the very late afternoon on the eve of the first qualifying round, and played six holes in street clothes. While Hagen was wrapping up his abbreviated practice round, Gene Sarazen was in the clubhouse sitting on a bench, soaking up the moment of being in the locker room at a major championship.

Gene wasn't the only professional adapting to being in the clubhouse at a major tournament; all the professional entrants were. At previous U.S. Open sites, amateurs like Bobby Jones would be welcomed with open arms into the clubhouse of the host venue, but the golf professionals in the field would have to remain outside. This attitude came along with the game's import from Great Britain, where the rigid class system there made it unthinkable for the elite to mix socially with the hired help at the grand old golf clubs.

As golf emerged in the United States, no one gave a thought to treating golf professionals any differently than they were treated in the game's place of origin. So for the first 25 years of U.S. Open history, rather than feeling like welcomed guests, players felt as if they were temporary inconveniences to the host course. The clubhouse and locker rooms were off limits. If they wanted to change clothes or out of their golf shoes after the round, they would have to do so in the parking lot or in the caddie shack. If they wanted food or liquid refreshment, they had to obtain it elsewhere.

Toledo did not match up with the social notions of previous Open locales like Boston, Newport, Philadelphia, and New York City. The driving force behind the effort to bring the Open to Toledo was S. P. Jermain. He was president of Inverness, and had been one of the game's biggest ambassadors in the Midwest. He was a civic leader in Toledo and very much the champion of the everyday man. He led the founding of the city's park system and championed establishing a municipal golf course in Toledo. It was one of the first such courses outside of the Northeast.

For its moment as the country's biggest golf stage, Inverness had built a grand new clubhouse. Jermain lobbied hard with the membership to allow golf professionals access to the clubhouse during the Open. They concurred. When the professionals arrived for the Open they were welcomed into the clubhouse with open arms. From that day forward, the golf professional, at least in the United States, was viewed in an entirely different light.

As the four days of competition were about to begin, there was no clear-cut favorite. The event was considered wide open. Although the return of Vardon and Ray to the U.S. Open field created plenty of buzz, they were not viewed with awe, as they had been before the 1913 Open. After all, Vardon was 50 years old and Ray, at 43, was no spring chicken. In the previous 24 U.S. Opens, no winner had been older than his early 30s.

Due to his tumble at the British Open, Hagen's chances were lumped in with a cluster of top-notch, home-bred players that included Jones; Chick Evans, who had won the U.S. Open and the U.S. Amateur in 1916; Leo Diegel, a superb ball striker; Mike Brady, who had finished second to Hagen at the 1919 U.S. Open; and William "Wild Bill" Melhorn out of Tulsa, Oklahoma, who was extra-long off the tee and an excellent putter.

Accommodating the record 278 entrants during qualifying was a challenge. Beginning at sunrise, twosomes were sent off every five minutes until 5:15 p.m. The big names received the more favorable times. Harry Vardon and Bobby Jones went off at 10:00 a.m., Hagen at 10:20, and Ray at 11:00.

The Vardon/Jones matchup drew the lion's share of the gallery on the first day. This pairing made quite a contrast, the aging king of golf and the 18-year-old prodigy who would one day wear that crown. The huge throng following them got to see the best and worst of young Bobby. After hitting a dismal short hook from the tee at the par-four fourth hole, Bobby reached the green and saved par with a stellar 2-wood shot from a punishing side-hill lie in the rough. At the fifth tee, Vardon would tell Bobby his 2-wood shot was one of the finest recovery shots he had ever witnessed.

On the back nine, a series of three putts activated Bobby's white-hot temper. At the 16th green, he totally lost it, hurling his putter off the green after tapping in his third putt. When the duo reached the scorer's tent, they each signed for 75. The next day, in the second round of qualifying, Jones bettered Vardon by two strokes, 76 to 78. Their scores put them in the top third of the 70 golfers who qualified (low 64 and ties). Ray and Hagen were in the bottom third of qualifiers, both making it into the field by just two strokes.

Grantland Rice's quest to make the Open field melted away in his opening round, when he shot an 89.

Jock Hutchison, a pro out of Chicago, was the low qualifier. A native of the home of golf, St. Andrews, Scotland, Hutchison had been in the United States for almost 20 years and had recently become a naturalized U.S. citizen. Despite his impressive performance, Hutchison found that he had to share the attention of the press with the third-place finisher. He was an 18-year-old long shot, and his name was Gene Sarazen.

2

DRIVER OFF THE DECK

Long before he struck the "shot heard 'round the world" at Augusta, Gene Sarazen was described by one of his contemporaries as a "publicity hound that was always in heat." Gene got his first dose of significant press exposure at the conclusion of the final qualifying round at Inverness. Surrounded by reporters and photographers, he basked in the moment.

Ironically, if most of his acquaintances from his old neighborhood and the countless golfers he had caddied for over the years read about the performance of Gene Sarazen in the qualifying round at Inverness, they would have been clueless as to who he was. They had known him as Eugenio Saraceni. A short time after he transitioned from the caddie ranks to the pro shop, Gene played a round with three friends. The first hole they played was a 145-yard par three. Gene's tee shot at the hole tracked the flag all the way and disappeared into the cup on its second bounce. A member of the group called in Gene's accomplishment to a local paper and they ran a short blurb about it in their next edition.

In 1950, Gene penned an autobiography with the assistance of noted golf writer Herbert Warren Wind titled *Thirty Years of Championship Golf*. In it, Gene recounted his hole-in-one and the displeasure he experienced in seeing his name in print on the sports page. His thinking was that Saraceni looked like the name of an opera singer or a school teacher. It did not roll off the tongue like the names of the three golfing stars of the day who were getting the most print in the papers—Chick Evans, Jim Barnes, and Hagen. He decided a name change was in order. He spent the next several weeks coming up with and testing names verbally and by penning them on paper. Beyond doubt, he believed he struck gold with Sarazen. It had zip and it proved to be quite unique, as a check of local phone books found no listings by that name. He furthermore decided that he was chucking Eugenio as well. Henceforth, he would go by Gene.

There well could have been another reason for the name change that Gene never disclosed. He may have wanted to put some distance between himself and his Italian heritage. Gene's parents had been part of a flood of Italian immigrants to the United States near the turn of the twentieth century. Most of the immigrants settled in metropolitan areas where work was more readily available. It wasn't long before few U.S. cities of any size in America did not have a section designated as Little Italy.

Many Americans were taken back by this huge influx, and a backlash in the form of discrimination against Italian Americans developed. Those who had problems with Italian immigrants considered them unintelligent menial laborers who were willing to work long hours for very little money. Many in the country's growing trade union movement believed the Italian immigrants were a threat to the American worker. A job posting during this period, for labor for the construction of reservoirs in the New York City area, reflects the attitude Italian immigrants faced: It read "whites would be paid from $1.30 to 1.50 a day, colored workers $1.25 to 1.40 and Italians $1.15 to 1.25."

In his early days in the caddie yard, Gene had faced this discrimination firsthand as he was often passed over in getting a bag because of a golfer's anti-Italian sentiment.

Twenty-four hours after being the darling of the press's attention at Inverness, Gene was the epitome of yesterday's news. In the morning 18 holes of that first day of the Open, he shot a 79. He matched that number in round two that afternoon. This left him 13 strokes out the lead heading into the final 36 holes on the last day, placing him well into the also-ran category. As that day unfolded, one of Gene's acquaintances from his caddie days was on center stage in the thick of the battle. This individual had not transitioned into a player; he was still carrying a bag. His name was Joe Horgan.

In the early 1890s, Horgan had begun caddying at St. Andrew's Golf Club in Yonkers, New York; this club's formation in 1888 had ignited the fuse that led to the golf explosion in the United States.

Due to a price war between shipping lines in the fall of 1895, Horgan was able to travel for a fare of 25 cents from New York City to Newport, Rhode Island, for the inaugural U.S. Open. The Newport Country Club was the host venue, and soon after arriving on its grounds, Horgan agreed to caddie for one of the 11 participants in the event, 19-year-old Horace Rawlins, who was the assistant pro at the Newport Country Club and a recent arrival from Scotland. The event was played in one day. It was 36 holes. Rawlins got off to a shaky start in the first 18, but caught fire in the final 18 to win by two strokes.

Soon after Joe returned to New York City, he changed his caddying base from St. Andrew's to the newly opened public course at Van Cortlandt Park, where, due to his duties with Rawlins at the Open, he was quite the celebrity. Horgan's stock continued to spiral upward. Over the next decade he would be the caddie for the U.S. Open winner on three more occasions.

Horgan was also the caddie for a number of winners of big-time amateur events for both men and women. When not working high-profile events, he kept busy working amateur events in and around New York City. One of the best players at the club where Gene caddied, the Apawamis Golf Club, played in these tournaments. In the last couple of years of Gene's caddying days, he would travel with him. It was at these events that Gene became acquainted with Joe, who took the younger caddies under his wing. When overnight stays were required, in most cases the caddies slept under the stars. In bad weather, Joe would find a place for the caddies to bunk down, either through contacts or by stealth in a barn or garage near the course.

At Inverness, Joe was on the bag of the highest profile golfer in the field, Harry Vardon. No one had expected Vardon to be a factor at Inverness. He was 50 years old. It was thought that he had made the trip over to make a farewell tour of the United States and to keep Ted Ray company. Those at Inverness were in a state of shock when Vardon reached the 12th tee in the final round with a five-stroke lead. But at this point, father time caught up with Vardon, and the wheels came off his game.

At the 17th hole, Harry was clinging to a one-stroke advantage. His drive had been far from his best. When the duo of the world's most accomplished golfer and America's top caddie reached the spot where Harry's drive had come to rest, they surveyed the situation. Harry faced a long difficult second shot, in which he would need to carry a ditch that guarded the front of the green. Joe Horgan advised Harry to lay up short of the ditch and try to make par with a good pitch and a one-putt. "Not now," said Harry. "I'd as well be in the ditch as short." A few moments later he went after his second shot with all he had. It wasn't enough. The ditch was just four feet across. Harry's ball came down right in its middle and he took a double bogey six.

Harry closed out his round with a par at the 18th and, with a wearisome gait, exited the green and headed for the scorer's tent. Ted Ray was still on the course. He had made a surge. His surge combined with Vardon's collapse had given him the lead by three strokes. A couple of late bogeys made things interesting, but Ray claimed the victory by one stroke with a two-putt par at the 18th.

Ray, 43 years and 16 days old, became the oldest player to win the U.S. Open. This record would stand until 1986, when Raymond Floyd won the Open at Shinnecock at the age of 43 years, 9 months, and 11 days. Floyd's mark would stand until the current holder of the record, Hale Irwin, won the 1990 Open at the age of 45 years and 15 days.

Had Vardon not stumbled down stretch at Inverness, a win at 50 years of age would not only still stand as a U.S. Open record; it would also stand as the record for any of golf's four major championships.

Gene played respectably during the final day's 36 holes, shooting 73s in both rounds to finish in 30th place. He received no respect, however, from the *New York Times*. Now one of the champions of political correctness, the paper went pretty low. It took Gene to task for his lack of stature—not figuratively but literally, describing him, at five feet, five inches, as one of three midgets in the field.

After Inverness, Gene returned to his assistant professional duties in Fort Wayne. In early 1921, he landed his first head pro position at the Titusville Country Club, 100 miles north of Pittsburgh.

In July, Gene journeyed to the Washington, DC, area to compete in the 1921 U.S. Open, taking place at the Columbia Country Club in Chevy Chase, Maryland. Since the beginning of the year, interest in the first Open to be played in the DC area had been building. It skyrocketed three weeks before the event, thanks to the outcome of that year's British Open.

The victory by Great Britain's Ted Ray at Inverness stung the nation's golf community. A concerted effort to regain, at the first opportunity, the prestige the Ouimet victory at Brookline had given the American golfer soon took shape. That first opportunity was at the 1921 British Open at the Old Course in St. Andrews, Scotland.

Previous American participation in the British Open had featured just a smattering of entries each year and had produced no significant impact. Soon after Ted Ray's win at Inverness, James Harnett, the circulation director of *Golf Illustrated* and *Outdoor Life*, spawned and spearheaded an effort to raise funds to underwrite sending a small army of American golf professionals to St. Andrews to represent the United States in what was then the world's premier golf event. Harnett's campaign sought contributions from golfers across the country and they responded. The final tally proved large enough to send a team of 12 golfers across the Atlantic.

The large-scale assault by American professionals created the most stir in the Open Championship's history. The headliners in the American group were Walter Hagen and Jock Hutchinson, the one member of the American team who would feel right at home in St. Andrews. As mentioned earlier, St. Andrews was Jock's birthplace and he had honed his golfing skills on the Old Course.

The year 1920 had been noteworthy for Jock. He became a naturalized citizen of the United States and finished in a four-way tie for second place at the U.S. Open at Inverness. And 10 days after Inverness, at the Chicago area's Flossmoor Country Club, he had claimed the Professional Golfers' Association (PGA) Championship.

In the Open Championship at St. Andrews, Jock gave all those American golfers who had underwritten the team's expenses the return on investment they desired. In the first round, he shot into contention, thanks to a hole-in-one. At the end of four rounds of regulation play, he and Britain's Roger Wethered were tied for first place. In a 36-hole play-off the next day, Jock crushed Wethered by 9 strokes.

Hutchison received quite the welcome when his ship docked in New York City and he came down the gangway carrying the famed Claret Jug, the 48-year-old trophy awarded to the winner of golf's most revered championship.

The country's golf fans were fired up over the prospect that Hutchison could become the first American to have won both Open titles and the first player to do so in the same year.

Instead of a two-day qualifier for the whole field as was used at Inverness, for this Open the USGA split the 263 entrants into two groups, with the top 35 in each group earning a spot in the event.

Jock Hutchison easily made the field, finishing fifth in the first qualifier. As he had at Inverness, Gene made a strong showing during qualifying, finishing fourth in the second day's qualifier.

Defending champion Ted Ray elected not to defend his title. Easily qualifying and carrying the hopes for Great Britain in this Open were George Duncan and Abe Mitchell. Duncan had won the 1920 British Open, coming from 13 strokes behind after two rounds, and Mitchell was one of the longest hitters on either side of the Atlantic.

The Columbia Country Club was a par 70. By the standards of the day, it was considered a superb test. A brutal summer heat wave had made it even more challenging, resulting in the greens being in a very parched state. In hopes of giving the putting surfaces some relief, they were powdered heavily with coal dust. This treatment, however, did not produce any improvement. Only two scores under par would be recorded during the entire event.

As at Inverness, Gene stumbled badly out of the gate. He was in the bottom third of the field after round one. He got back on his game in round two, while Jock had a train wreck in the second round and fell far back in the pack. He would remain there for the rest of the tournament.

In rounds three and four, Gene was paired with Bobby Jones, who had posted one of the top scores in round two, a one over par 71. This was the first time the two had made each other's acquaintance. They each shot 77 in both rounds. Bobby's final round 77 could have been much better had he not driven his ball out of bounds twice from the fifth tee, which led to a nine on the hole. Gene finished the Open in the 17th spot. Bobby took fifth.

The two stars from England had mixed results. Like Hutchison, Mitchell had a disastrous second round. Midway through his back nine, he picked up his ball and stormed back to the clubhouse. Duncan, on the other hand, played well throughout the four rounds and finished in a tie for second place, but he was nine strokes behind the winner, Jim Barnes. Walter Hagen tied Duncan for second place. Walter had bested Barnes by one stroke over the last 54 holes but his first round had been a disaster. While Barnes posted a 69 in that round, Walter shot a 79.

Barnes was a native of England but he had been in the States for almost 20 years. His win was far from a surprise, as he had won the PGA Championship in 1916 and 1919.

Two months later, the PGA Championship kicked off at the Inwood Country Club on Long Island. As it was at its inception and how it would remain until 1958, the PGA Championship was a match play event. Over the years, the length of the matches would vary from 18 to 36 holes. At the 1921 event, all the matches were scheduled for 36 holes. Jock Hutchison started the defense of his title with an easy victory in the first round. On the second day, his opponent was the Titusville Country Club's upstart professional. Gene had made it into the field by winning his sectional qualifier and had won his first-round match by a comfortable margin.

In their match, Jock won the second hole. It would be the only hole he would win during the first 18 holes. He would lose nine.

On the front nine at the Inwood Country Club holes three, four, and five are consecutive par fives. As that fateful day at Augusta National would bear out, Gene played his best golf on par-fives. At the third hole, he made birdie to square the match. He then birdied four and five. Gene's par-five birdie barrage staggered Hutchison. By the completion of their first 18 holes, the Inwood course was buzzing over what had happened in their match. The British Open champion and defending PGA champion was eight down to a 19-year-old.

The afternoon 18 of the Hutchison/Sarazen match drew most of the fans and all of the press. Hutchison made a strong effort to at least make the margin more respectable. He birdied the three par fives on the front, but unfortunately, Jock lost ground, as Gene birdied two of those par fives and eagled the other one. Over the remaining holes, Jock won two and Gene one. The match ended when they halved the 11th hole, with Gene holding an eight-up advantage with seven to play.

In the press tent, Gene's victory over Jock Hutchison was being heralded as the golf story of the year. Gene had received a small dose of the limelight at Inverness with his unexpected strong showing in the qualifying round. His win over Hutchison, however, gave him an overdose of the limelight and he did not handle it well. Gene came across as brash and cocky in his post-match interactions with the press and fans, leaving many turned off by his attitude.

Gene's time in the spotlight was short-lived. In his third round match against Cyril Walker, a future U.S. Open winner, he experienced an almost complete reversal of fortune. He was over par on the par fives and at one point in the match he had a stretch of four consecutive bogeys. The match ended at the 32nd hole with Walker five-up and Gene headed back to Titusville.

One of the ironies of being a golf professional during this period was that one week your name would be splattered all over the newspapers, and the next week you would be doling out tee times in a pro shop. Shortly after the PGA Championship, it was a tee-time dispute that ended Gene's employment in Titusville. A member's son did not like the starting time Gene gave him and words were exchanged. One thing led to another, and soon the two were behind the pro shop exchanging blows. According to Gene, he was the victor, but he knew what the final result would be. Instead of waiting to be fired, he quit.

A few months after his departure from Titusville, Gene headed south to play the winter circuit, which kicked off in Texas and then worked its way over to Florida and then north through Georgia and the Carolinas. He finished high in several early events. At about the midway point of the circuit, he picked up his first win, the Southern Open in New Orleans, in more than impressive fashion, winning by a nine-stroke margin over a stout field.

While the circuit was on its Florida swing, Gene accepted an offer to become the head professional at the soon-to-be-opened Highland Country Club just outside Pittsburgh.

By the time the tour headed for its last stop, the North-South Open in Pinehurst, Gene had compiled an impressive record. To go with his win at New Orleans, he registered three second-place and two fourth-place finishes. While none of his peers could question his talent, many were put off by Gene's cocky and brash attitude and short-fused temper. A temper tantrum ended his winter tour experience a day early. Gene could not adjust to Pinehurst No. 2's sand greens. He picked up his ball and stomped off the course during round two, drawing an abundance of criticism from his fellow players and the press.

The 1922 U.S. Open was scheduled for mid-July at the Skokie Country Club in Glencoe, Illinois, just north of Chicago. The Highland Country Club was very supportive of Gene playing in the Open, and allowed him to take a week off in June to go up to the Skokie club for practice rounds.

Ten days before the Open at Skokie was to commence, a great wave of patriotism took place on a dock in New York City. Waving American flags and red, white, and blue streamers, a huge throng gathered. The U.S.

Army's Seventh Regiment Band was there, delivering a spirited perfor-mance. It had all the patriotic fervor of a July Fourth celebration, but the Fourth was still three days away. This crowd was there to afford what the press would call the greatest welcome ever afforded a returning athlete. As the band belted out "Hail the Conquering Hero," Walter Hagen, the winner of the 1922 British Open at Royal St. George's at Sandwich by one stroke, came down the ocean liner's ramp with the Claret Jug in his hands.

Although Jock Hutchison's win the year before had been significant, he was not, as the popular term of the day defined it, a home-bred. Hagen was. The Rochester, New York, native's victory in golf's oldest and most prestigious championship had ignited tremendous national pride. The prospect of an American, a home-bred one, winning both the British Open and the U.S. Open brought interest in America's golf championship to an all-time level.

The Skokie Country Club had opened in 1897 as a nine-hole course. In 1904 the old course gave away to a new 18-hole course. In 1914 the membership decided that their course needed to be upgraded, and brought Donald Ross up from Pinehurst to redesign the layout. Ross turned in his usual outstanding performance. When the 1922 U.S. Open was awarded to Skokie, it marked the third time in four years the event would be held on a course redesigned by Ross.

In mid-May the Skokie Country Club was in marvelous shape, but then Mother Nature got a little testy. When the Open week arrived, the Chicago area had endured a stretch of 45 days without rain. The fairways at Skokie were burned out and the greens were rock-hard. Again, the Open drew a record number of entrants, 329. This large number forced the USGA to go with three days of qualifying. On each of the three days, one-third of the entrants played 36 holes with finishers in the top 25 spots and ties making the field. Fortunately during these three days, relief from the drought arrived. A light rain fell off and on during the first two days of qualifying, and on the third day of qualifying the bottom fell out in the early afternoon, forcing a suspension of play for the day. This moved the start of the Open back one day.

George Duncan and Abe Mitchell were again representing Great Brit-ain in the field. Mitchell easily qualified, but Duncan struggled. Playing in the third-day qualifier, he was on the bubble for most of his second 18 that day, but ultimately made it in by two strokes.

Duncan finished 10 strokes behind the leader of that day's qualifier, who was his playing partner, Walter Hagen. Walter had played his round without going to the practice tee. As was his trademark, he was often late for his tee time and this day had been no exception. His arrival at the first tee had been further delayed by a conscientious gate attendant. The 1922 Open was the first time there was an admission charged. It was one dollar. When Hagen attempted to enter the grounds, he was stopped by the attendant and asked to produce a ticket. He advised the attendant that he was a contestant. He was then asked to produce his player's badge. Walter didn't have it on him. He was on the way to the box office to pay his one-dollar admission fee when a USGA official spotted him. Luckily for Walter, the USGA was not as stringent as it would later be about being on time. This official had been dispatched to find Walter because he and Duncan were the marquee pairing of the day and they had been scheduled to tee off 20 minutes earlier. The official grabbed Walter and ushered him by the attendant and straight to the first tee.

This year's Open, as in the past, was a two-day affair with 36 holes played each day. Gene and Bobby Jones had both easily qualified for their third U.S. Open attempts. At the end of day one, Gene and Walter were three shots off the lead in a tie for third. One stroke behind them was Jones, who was alone in fourth. The surprise leader was John L. Black, the pro at the Claremont Club in Oakland, California. A 44-year-old grandfather, Black, a native of Scotland, had started in golf as a caddie, become a professional, then given it up to be a carpenter for a number of years before returning to the game.

In his first round, Black moved into serious contention with back-to-back birdies at 14 and 15. On the 14th hole, a 315-yard par four, he drove the green. This created quite a buzz through the gallery and he became the Cinderella story of the event. He finished the day with a two-shot lead. Wild Bill Melhorn, from nearby Elgin, Illinois, was alone in second, two strokes back.

On day two, Gene started his third round with a substantial following. But by the time he holed out at the ninth hole, there were just a few followers left. Gene had shot a dismal 40 on the front and with each bogey a portion of his gallery had peeled away. He settled down on his back nine and came home even par. He started his afternoon 18 with a sterling front-side score of 33, which would be the lowest score turned in on that side during the entire tournament. This placed him in a three-way race with Bobby Jones and John Black for the championship.

When Gene reached the par-five 18th hole, he believed his chances for victory hinged on his making a birdie there. His drive was just average. This left him with a huge decision for his second shot. He was unsure his 3-wood would get him to the green. His other option was to lay up and play for a pitch-and-putt birdie.

Since this was long before golfers had their own personal caddies, hordes of caddies had shown up at Skokie, hoping to get a bag in the Open. The caddie master assigned a fellow Italian to Gene, a young lad named Domenico. Where Gene was torn as to what to do on his second shot, Domenico was not. He urged Gene to go for it and he won Gene over. As to the club, Gene was still of the opinion that the 3-wood would not get him there; he asked Domenico for his driver.

In a parallel to his Augusta National shot, few people would witness this driver-off-the-deck blow that would in the end prove to be the winning shot. His timing and rhythm on the execution of the shot could not have been better. The ball was short on altitude but had loads of juice. Although it landed well short of the green, it had plenty of roll that carried his ball onto the green and into makeable eagle-putt range. But that type of ending at the 72nd hole of a U.S. Open was not in the cards on this day. His putt-for-eagle effort was just off line. When Gene tapped in his birdie putt, he was the leader in the clubhouse, unseating Bill Melhorn, who had grabbed the lead a few minutes earlier when he holed a pitch shot at 18 for an eagle.

While Gene signed his card for a 68, the lowest final round ever in a U.S. Open, still out on the course were Bobby Jones and John Black. Black was at 15 and Jones was teeing off on 18. Black was tied with Gene, and Jones was one stroke back.

Jones needed an eagle at 18 to vault over Gene; birdie would put him in a tie. He got neither. He was well in range of the par five's green after his drive, but his 3-wood approach was well off line. He could not get up and down and had to settle for a par.

At 15, Black made a sensational up and down from 50 yards to save par. His birdie putt at 16 from 20 feet was dead in the heart, but three inches short. At the par-four 17th, disaster struck. Black, who was on the cusp of being the oldest player ever to win the Open, made his worst swing of the week. It sailed out of bounds and he took a double-bogey six.

Black now needed an eagle at 18 to force a play-off. He made the trek from the 17th green to the 18th tee without showing any outward signs of the dire situation that now faced him. Black had played the entire Open with a pipe in his mouth. Before he hit his drive, he paused and re-lit it. His effort off the tee was solid. His 3-wood second shot reached the green and left him a 40-footer for eagle and a tie.

Puffing on his pipe, Black took his time studying the line. His effort had the line all the way, but not the speed. He tapped in for birdie.

At the awards ceremony 15 minutes later, Gene was presented with the U.S. Open trophy. A chair was provided for him to stand on and address the throng that had gathered for the presentation.

It would likely be the only time for the rest of his life that Gene would be almost at a loss for words. After a few moments of uncomfortable silence he muttered, "I can't say anything, fellows; it's all in my heart and nothing is in my head."

3

ONE OF A KIND

Several hours after the awards ceremony at Skokie, Gene Sarazen took an overnight train back to Pittsburgh. At mid-morning the next day, he entered the grounds of the Highland Country Club; the caddies in the caddie yard saw him first and stampeded over to congratulate him. A few minutes later the president of the club, H. F. Hetzel, joined the impromptu welcome-home celebration. Gene had been away from his job for almost two weeks and was uncomfortable making another request for time off. But he really wanted to get back to the New York City area to share his victory with his friends and family. With unease, he made a request to Hetzel for two or three more days off for that purpose. Hetzel's response was for Gene to take another full week off.

Shortly before noon that day, Dutch Loeffler, the course superintendent at the Oakmont Country Club, arrived to take Gene to lunch. Loeffler competed with some regularity on the tournament circuit, and he had become acquainted with Gene when they took part in some of the same events. Loeffler, like Sarazen, had started in golf as a caddie at a very young age. When he was 17, he became caddie master at Oakmont. By the time he turned 21, he was the club's greenskeeper. Several years later he became Oakmont's course superintendent and also began to contract out his services as a course designer. The Highland Country Club was one of over 20 courses he would lay out over his career. Loeffler had recommended Gene for the job of Highland's golf professional.

For lunch that day, Dutch took Gene over to Oakmont where they dined with the king and prince of the Pittsburgh golf community: Henry

Clay Fownes and his son, William Clark Fownes Jr. The senior Fownes, a very successful iron manufacturer, did not take up golf until he was in his 40s. But when he did, he went all in. Fownes did not care for the high society atmosphere of existing country clubs in Pittsburgh, so he designed, built, and maintained the controlling interest in Oakmont Country Club. The senior Fownes also competed in the U.S. Amateur five times. Son William competed in the U.S. Amateur 19 times and was the winner of the event in 1910. He would later serve as president of the USGA.

Gene boarded a late train that evening and arrived at New York City's Penn Station the next morning. With his golf clubs slung over his shoulder and his travel bag in one hand and the U.S. Open trophy in the other, Gene headed for the city's palatial Biltmore Hotel. Gene drew plenty of stares as he trudged across the Biltmore's lobby to the front desk to register. He set his bags on the floor and gingerly placed the trophy on the counter.

Word of Sarazen's arrival quickly spread, and in a couple of hours he was back in the Biltmore's lobby with the trophy. Surrounded by reporters and photographers, he described in detail his victory at Skokie.

Upon his triumphant return to the New York City area, one would have thought Gene would head straight for his parent's home, but that was not the case. After holding court with the press at the Biltmore, Gene grabbed his trophy and headed for the Brooklawn Country Club in Bridgeport, Connecticut, to see his golf father, George Sparling.

It was at the Brooklawn Club a few years earlier that Gene had received his big break. A golf professional at a local municipal course in Bridgeport had taken an interest in Gene's desire to join the golf profession. He told him that George Sparling over at Brooklawn might have a slot, and he arranged an interview for Gene with Sparling.

Initially, Sparling was not impressed with Gene. He was of the opinion that caddies wanting to move up were a dime a dozen. At this time, with World War I winding down, Sparling was expecting that soon there would be a rich pool of applicants emigrating from Scotland with more knowledge and skills.

Gene was persistent. He made repeated trips to Brooklawn to try and convince Sparling to hire him, but Sparling continued to give him the cold shoulder. One day after receiving another rejection, Gene was observed behind the Brooklawn clubhouse swinging a club by two of Brooklawn's most influential members. The two were brothers. They struck up a conversation with Gene and learned of his desire to work at the club. The brothers took a shine to Gene and prevailed upon Sparling to give him a shot at the job, which was a combination pro shop attendant, apprentice club maker, and janitor.

Throughout Sarazen's career in golf, his biggest moments seemed to take place at par fives. The first of these notable par-five moments occurred soon after his employment began at the Brooklawn Country Club. With member pressure the reason for his hire, Sparling's treatment of Gene was quite frosty. This soon changed thanks to one of Brooklawn's par fives.

One afternoon during a driving rainstorm, Sparling, several members, and a couple of pros from other clubs were having a bull session in the pro shop. At some point, their conversation turned to the difficulty of various holes at clubs in the area. Sparling brought up the stoutness of Brooklawn's long par-five fourth hole and how difficult it was to reach its green in two shots. Gene had been monitoring the conversation from his work area and instantly piped up. "Boss, I will bet you five I can get home there in two." Sparling glared at Gene with contempt and took the bet.

Gene grabbed his driver and he and George Sparling and several others from the group piled into a car and drove to the fourth tee. Gene teed up his ball in the pouring rain and ripped a long drive down the fairway. He then scampered back to the vehicle and was driven down to near his ball. After drying off his hands and the grip of his driver as best he could, Gene raced back into the rain and powdered his second shot. To the amazement of Sparling and the other occupants of the vehicle, Gene's ball landed deep into the green.

In his position, Gene was working 60 plus hours a week for a salary of $8. In 15 minutes' time he had increased his income for that week by over 50 percent, but more importantly, he had established with Sparling that he was not in the dime-a-dozen class. He was one of a kind. From that point forward, Sparling treated Gene more like a son than an employee, earnestly imparting his knowledge of the finer points of the game to him.

After his visit with Sparling and some time spent with his parents, Gene concluded his stay by playing in several exhibition matches in the New York City area. When he returned to Pittsburgh, he was greeted not like someone who had only lived in the area for four months, but as a conquering native son. In the spacious ballroom at the city's William

Penn Hotel, a gathering of almost a thousand attended a dinner in his honor. Gifts, which included a gold watch, were lavished on him.

Pittsburgh had long been one of the country's hotbeds for golf, and it was all abuzz about its adopted favorite son's prospects in the upcoming PGA Championship, which was to be held at the Oakmont Country Club in less than a month. Adding more fire to the building anticipation for the PGA was the possibility of a head-to-head match-up between the reigning U.S. Open Champion and its defending champion and current British Open champion, Walter Hagen. But Hagen soon doused that prospect when he announced that he was going to skip the PGA Championship in favor of playing in a string of lucrative exhibition matches.

In the PGA, Sarazen laid to rest any speculation that his win at the U.S. Open had been a fluke. The field was divided into four 16-man brackets. Gene moved through his bracket with relative ease. In these four matches, only the third was a tight contest. It was against Jock Hutchison, the man he had trampled in the event the year before. This time it was a nip-and-tuck affair until Gene put on a closing spurt to take the match three and one.

In his semifinal, Gene polished off Bobby Cruickshank three and two, and then beat Emmet French in the final in convincing fashion, four and three. In doing so, Gene became the youngest player ever to win the PGA and the first player to capture the U.S. Open and the PGA Championship in the same year.

At the awards dinner at Oakmont that evening, there was a big announcement—a showdown match, dubbed the "Unofficial World Championship of Golf," between Gene and Walter Hagen had been arranged. It would take place in six weeks in early October. The format would be match play. It would take place over two days at two different locales with 36 holes being contested each day. Oakmont would host the first day, which was to take place on a Friday. Soon after the conclusion of those 36 holes, the two players would board a train and travel to New York City to conclude the match the next day at the Westchester-Biltmore Country Club.

On that historic day at Augusta in 1935, as Gene addressed his ball and prepared to send into flight the most famous golf shot in history, he could not have asked for anything more than to have Walter Hagen standing just a few yards away from him, observing the moment.

Hagen and Sarazen were the combatants in American professional golf's first great rivalry. The two were polar opposites. Hagen stood over six feet and towered over the five-foot-five Sarazen. Walter had a peculiar lurching stroke and was wildly inconsistent off the tee, but was a superb scrambler. He had serious disdain for the practice range. Asked about this aversion, he once said, "Why waste good shots there that you may need on the course." Gene on the other hand had one of the game's most polished swings and worked extra hard on the range maintaining it. His tee to green play was a model of consistency.

When it came to pace of play, Gene was a sprinter. Walter bounced back and forth between being a hare or a tortoise. His tortoise pace often involved his adding showmanship or drama to the shot he was facing. Much to the irritation of his playing partners and opponents, he would often over ponder the simplest of shots, while feigning wiping perspiration from his brow.

Walter's most noted theatrical presentation came on his 72nd hole at the British Open at Royal St. Annes in 1926. Before he teed off on the par-four hole, he was apprised that he would need to make an eagle two in order to catch Bobby Jones, who was the leader in the clubhouse and ultimate winner. Walter ripped a good drive and had about 155 yards left to the pin. Before playing the shot, he made the long walk up to the green and surveyed the pin's location, while the throng packed around the green and lining both sides of the fairway looked on. Upon completing his analysis, Walter instructed a tournament official to have the pin removed and walked slowly back down the fairway to his ball. When his shot came off the clubface, it was definitely tracking for the cup's location. It landed just two feet from the flagless hole but bounded by and scooted off the back of the green. Walter took four more shots to get down for a double-bogey six.

When it came to handling money, Gene was always focused on having financial security. Walter was not. He spent money as fast as he could earn it, often much faster. His lifestyle of lavish living, drinking, and womanizing easily made him a top candidate for the poster boy of the Roaring Twenties.

Interest in the Sarazen/Hagen match-up was very high from the outset and ticked up daily over the next six weeks. It was soon being referred to as the most anticipated golf match in the country's history. Bookies were doing a booming business. Most were giving the edge to Hagen, but only slightly.

During the run-up to their match, Gene became annoyed by the amount of press coverage Walter's wardrobe received. Walter made his first appearance at a U.S. Open at Brookline in 1913. He finished in a four-way tie for fourth place, three strokes out of the Ouimet, Vardon, and Ray play-off. At Brookline, Walter was very impressed by another golfer in that field, Tom Anderson, Jr. Anderson came from a long line of golfing professionals in Scotland, but it wasn't his game that impressed Walter. It was his attire. Anderson wore silk shirts, colorful bandannas, and flashy shoes. In short order, Walter began to emulate Anderson's dress. He started slowly with bandanas. A year later, adorned in a green one, he won the U.S. Open at the Midlothian Country Club outside of Chicago. With his pockets deepened, he began to divert a large portion of his income to his wardrobe. Colorful silk shirts, striped pants, and flashy golf shoes became his trademark.

The word matching would be a stretch on many of Walter's wardrobe combinations, if they had been worn by anyone else. But for some reason, on Walter they looked like the epitome of good fashion. When Gene had recorded his breakthrough victory earlier in 1922 at the Southern Open in New Orleans, a photo taken of him showed his attire was a long way from matching up with his first-class swing. Several weeks later as the winter tour made its way through Florida, a very attractive young woman pulled Gene aside in a hotel lobby. Her name was Consuelo, and she was the wife of another budding young star on the American golf scene, Tommy Armour. Although Tommy's style wasn't as showy as Walter Hagen's, he was a classy dresser on the course. Consuelo wanted to talk to Gene about his attire on the course, and she was pretty blunt. She told Gene he looked like a caddie and then gave him the contact information for the gentleman who provided most of her husband's golfing apparel.

Financially, Gene had struck out on the winter tour that season on a wing and a prayer. Travel, lodging, and meal money were his paramount concerns. His wardrobe on and off the course was bare bones. To increase his odds of surviving the 15-week circuit, he and four other golfers formed a syndicate. At the end of an event, all their winnings would be combined and divided five ways. The first-place purse for his win at the Southern Open was $1,000. Unfortunately for Gene, the four other members of the syndicates all finished out of the money and he netted only two hundred dollars from his first tour win. He pulled out of the syndicate at that point.

High finishes in the next two events improved his financial situation enough that he indulged himself a little on clothes, but it was on street clothes. In Mobile, Alabama, he strolled into a tailor shop and bought his first suit—a brown tweed. It was soon after that purchase that he had the conversation with Consuela Armour, and he began to concentrate on improving his on-the-course appearance. Like it had done for Walter Hagen, Gene's win at the U.S. Open opened up many other financial opportunities, allowing him to focus on his on- and off-the-course wardrobes in a big way.

Although the press coverage of their impending showdown was close to even in regard to the two golfers' playing ability, seldom did a piece not include a reference to Hagen being the game's most well-dressed golfer. Gene, already ticked at Walter for constantly referring to him as "The Kid" or "Junior," let it be known that when their match began at Oakmont, not only would his game be up to Walter's, but his wardrobe would be as well.

In his practice rounds before their showdown, Gene's caddie pulled double duty as his valet, carrying his golf bag and a box of sweaters. Gene had developed a thing for sweaters, sweaters that had a Persian rug look. Since it was barely into the fall the weather was still warm, and when the sweater he had on became soaked with perspiration, he would request a fresh one from his caddie.

Gene's penchant for the Persian rug-looking sweater would soon fade, but what he had recently taken to wearing below his waist would not. According to press accounts, co-runner-up John Black had been the only player at the U.S. Open at Skokie who wore knickers. Shortly after his win there, Gene had slipped into a pair of knickers. From that point forward, knickers became his trademark. He never set foot on a golf course in anything else. He often boasted of his collection of knickers that at its peak totaled over 100, with matching long stockings. Soon after Gene began wearing them, knickers became a hot item for golfers, and they remained a hot item until the early 1930s when, except for Gene and a handful of others, they fell out of fashion. When it was announced that the maker of the long stockings was going to soon cease operation, Gene rushed out an order for 400 pair.

In their top-drawer attire, Sarazen and Hagen stepped onto the first tee at the Oakmont Country Club for the opening 36 holes of the match.

Constructed in 1903, Oakmont was considered the most challenging course in America, and the argument can be made that it still holds that distinction today. Its record as a championship venue is unsurpassed. As of this writing, it has hosted the U.S. Open nine times, three PGA Championships, five U.S. Amateurs, and two Women's U.S. Opens.

By the time Sarazen and Hagen struck their opening drives, the number in attendance rivaled that of a U.S. Open and those numbers continued to build well into the afternoon round. Controlling the throng was as challenging for the course's marshals as the Oakmont layout was for the two golfers. They were all in for Gene, and they responded to Walter like a Hatfield would respond to a McCoy. When Walter hit a good shot there would hardly be a murmur through the crowd. When his ball found a trap or he missed a putt, they cheered. It was the total opposite when it came to Gene. They cheered his every shot, even if it was mishit or found a bunker.

If Hagen was bothered by the allegiance of the crowd, it did not show. He jumped out to a quick two-up lead at the outset and kept Gene at bay through the morning round. In the afternoon 18, Walter began to steadily pull away. A win at the 11th hole gave him a five-up advantage and turned the raucous pro-Sarazen crowd into the equivalent of a mournful funeral procession.

Gene breathed a bit of life into his followers with a win at 12. He then took 13 and then 14 and by this point the crowd had been fully resurrected and was cheering him on with great fervor. Hagen managed to quell their enthusiasm by getting a half at the 15th hole. But Gene recharged the crowd when he grabbed another win at 16 to shave Walter's lead down to just one hole.

Gene's drive at the par-four, 282-yard 17th hole sent the gallery into a state of pandemonium when it rolled onto the green and came to rest some 60 feet from the cup. Another roar went up a few minutes later, when Walter attempted to reach the green as well and his ball strayed into a greenside bunker, leaving him a lengthy sand shot.

One would have thought at this point it would be a safe bet that the match was going to the last hole of the day all square. But as would be the case throughout the prime of his career, there were no safe bets when

Walter Hagen was involved. His long bunker blast landed like a boulder just a few feet from the hole.

Hagen's bunker shot must have rattled Gene. His putt for eagle was woefully misjudged, and his birdie attempt stayed out of the hole as well. He tapped in for par. Hagen drained his two-footer for birdie to go back to two-up. The last hole was halved.

Several hours later the two golfers boarded a train for the overnight run to New York City. There wasn't much sleep for Gene during that night on the rails. He was having sharp stomach pains that he attributed to a poor dinner choice.

When the train pulled into the station in New York City at around 8:00 the next morning, Gene and Walter were hustled into a waiting car. Under escort by police motorcycle officers with sirens blaring, they were whisked out to Westchester-Biltmore Country Club in Rye, New York.

The site of the final 36 holes of their match was considered a stiff test of golf. A par-75 layout, it featured highly elevated tees and greens with fairways bordered by deep ravines. It was not heavily trapped, however; it featured an abundance of natural hazards.

Given his great interest and passion for the game—and the added fact that in addition to his syndicated column workload, he had recently taken over as editor of the *American Golfer* magazine—one would have suspected that Grantland Rice, who was based in New York City, would have been trooping along with the gallery following Hagen and Sarazen at Westchester. But the Unofficial World Championship of Golf had picked the wrong weekend for the vast majority of sports fans in the country. It was butting heads against the World Series. The New York Giants were playing Babe Ruth and the New York Yankees in game four of the Series at the Polo Grounds in Upper Manhattan. Rice was there and he was multitasking again, not only covering the Series for his readers but doing play-by-play on the radio.

Both game four of the World Series and the final rounds of the Unofficial World Championship of Golf would be played in less-than-ideal conditions. On the first tee, Hagen and Sarazen were greeted by low-hanging clouds and a misty rain. This was as good as it was going to get. As the day progressed, the misty rain turned into showers and eventually a steady rain.

With the results from Oakmont carrying over, Gene started the day two-down, but he didn't stay that way for long. Walter apparently left his

"A" game in Pittsburgh. Gene was consistently outdriving him, and Walter's irons also lacked the crispness they had possessed the previous day. His putting was off as well. After the morning 18, Gene had erased his two-hole deficit and had taken a two-up lead.

Gene had dealt with two distractions during the morning 18. First, he had continued to have flashes of the same type of stomach pain he had experienced on the train ride from Pittsburgh. His second distraction was that he was constantly scanning the gallery to look for a special fan—a blonde.

Hagen's game had not been the only thing fading in the misty rain during the morning round; so had the orange-and-white tie Gene was wearing, a gift from that special fan. During the time between his win at the PGA and his match with Hagen, Gene had played several exhibition matches in and around New York City. While in the area, he had taken in some quality New York City nightlife. One of his stops had been at the Ziegfeld Follies, which featured a chorus line of beautiful leggy young ladies called the Ziegfeld Girls.

When Gene had arrived at the course that day, he was given a small package that had been left for him earlier that morning. He opened it and found the orange-and-white tie with a note requesting Gene to wear the tie in the match for good luck. The writer said she was a Ziegfeld Girl with blonde hair, and that she had spoken with him briefly during one of his visits at the Follies.

At the conclusion of the morning 18, most of the orange part of the tie had bled onto Gene's shirt. During lunch in the clubhouse, Walter remarked about the tie and then let be known that he had been its sender. It was a typical Hagen prank. It made Gene furious—not at Hagen, but at himself for falling for it, hook, line, and sinker.

Hagen sent a stir through the crowd on the first hole on the afternoon round, when he drove the green on the 280-yard par four and made a two-putt birdie to cut Gene's lead to one. But at the par-five 13th hole, Gene drained a 45-footer for eagle to regain a two-up lead. Several more times during the second 18, Walter would appear to be rallying, but each time Gene would snuff out his hopes. He closed Hagen out at the 34th hole to become golf's "Unofficial World Champion."

In the newspapers the next day, Gene's win received almost as much space as the Giants' 4–3 win over the Yankees in game four of the World Series. The following day the Giants took game five and the Series with a

5–3 win. Of course, their win dominated the sports pages the next day, but a story about Gene was also getting plenty of coverage, and it had nothing to do with his golf game.

At about the time the last out was made in the final game of the World Series, Gene was on a gurney being wheeled into surgery. The night of his victory, Gene's stomach pain intensified and he had to excuse himself from a dinner in his honor at the Westchester-Biltmore and go to his room. Two doctors were at the dinner and they went to Gene's room to check on him. After doing so, they believed that the rigors of the last two days were the culprit. They were of the opinion that a good night's rest was all Gene needed. That night, Gene got very little rest as the pain continued. The next day he sought out another doctor. This doctor had Gene rushed to St. John's Riverside Hospital. By mid-afternoon, he was on an operating table, having his appendix removed.

Gene was in the hospital for eight days. His appendix would stay there for at least another thirty years, as the *Washington Post* reported in 1952 that the hospital was still in possession of it and had it on display.

After his release from the hospital, Gene was provided accommodations at the Westchester-Biltmore to complete his recuperation. His recovery progress was followed intently in the press.

A week after he was given a clean bill of health, Gene was again in the news and again it had nothing to do with his golf game. As he was driving through White Plains, New York, one evening, an elderly man stepped out in front him and was severely injured. The man succumbed to those injuries three days later.

Soon after the accident, Gene was dealt another blow—this one related to golf. He was out of a job. The Highlands Country Club announced they were no longer in need of his services. The two parties had been negotiating for several weeks. Gene was requesting a hefty raise. He had also let it be known that after defeating Hagen, he planned to compete in the British Open. The amount of time this would require Gene to be away from his post in prime golf season was a problem for Highlands. The negotiations were not proceeding to either party's satisfaction. Highlands decided that they would cut Gene loose and issued a press release, citing the reason as their desire to have a professional who would devote the majority of his time to their members and the operation of the club. They made this announcement without notifying Gene first, which incensed him.

4

BEWARE OF WHAT YOU PRAY FOR

Gene Sarazen finished out 1922 playing exhibition matches, holding clinics, and weighing job offers from other country clubs. His schedule took him to Washington, DC, where he received an invitation to meet with one of that city's most avid golfers, President Warren Harding, at his residence.

Gene gained access to the White House because of his golf. It could be said that President Harding was there in spite of his golf.

Both Sarazen and President Harding had experienced their breakthrough moment in the Chicago area: Gene's, when he claimed the U.S. Open at Skokie. Harding's moment came in a smoke-filled hotel room in Chicago in July 1920 during the Republican Party's convention when, in the wee hours of the morning, the party's bosses decided on him as the GOP nominee for president.

Mere weeks after the convention, Harding's campaign was in a tailspin and an urgent call for assistance was placed to Chicago. The call wasn't being made to the party bosses; Harding's campaign was far beyond their help. It needed the Chicago Cubs.

Harding had ingested a huge dose of political poison—he had allowed himself to be filmed playing golf by a crew from a newsreel service. In 1920, golf was gaining steam in its popularity, particularly in certain pockets of the country, but its image with the overall population was very negative, as it was generally viewed as a game for the privileged.

As soon as the newsreel footage began to roll in movie houses around the country, the Harding campaign was inundated with negative reactions. Harding's team feverishly put together a plan to stage an event that they believed would be the perfect antidote for the golf film. They were going to put Harding back in front of the cameras, enjoying a game that was as mainstream America as you could get—baseball. The owner of the Chicago Cubs was a Harding backer, and arrangements were made with him to bring the Cubs to the candidate's hometown of Marion, Ohio, for a game against a team of locals.

The campaign ran stories a few days before the game about Harding's love for baseball. The pieces chronicled Harding's playing days as a bare-handed first baseman, and detailed how he was once a major stockholder in a professional team in the Ohio State League.

A crowd of 7,000 packed the small Marion ballpark and gave Harding a rousing welcome when he arrived. With the cameras rolling, Harding went straight onto the field and warmed up the Cubs' pitcher, future Hall of Famer Grover Cleveland Alexander. After the warm-up session, Harding made a few brief remarks to the crowd, threw out the game's ceremonial first ball, and then whooped it up in the grandstand like the contest was the seventh game of the World Series. The Cubs won the game 3–1, but Harding was the real winner. The game received generous nationwide newspaper coverage. When the newsreel footage reached the movie houses, reaction to it was what Harding's staffers had hoped it would be. They were confident that it more than cancelled out the negative effects of their candidate's golfing footage.

For the rest of the campaign, Harding golfed in secret. He went on to win the presidency in a landslide, defeating Democrat James Cox by almost a two-to-one margin in the popular vote and by almost a three-to-one margin in the Electoral College. A few days after the election, Harding headed to Florida for a lengthy golf vacation.

Harding's game was in the duffer class. He shot in the 90's and, like most golfers in this category, he could have used a little more distance off the tee. Hoping to assist the president in this regard, Gene gave him the driver he had used in winning the Open at Skokie.

From Washington, Sarazen returned to the New York City area for more clinics and exhibitions. During this time, he and Jock Hutchison put together a winter tour of the West Coast. Three days before their Christmas Day departure, it was announced that Gene had found a new golf home. He would become the golf professional for the Briarcliff Lodge, a luxury resort 30 miles outside of New York City in Westchester County.

Previously, Briarcliff had been a golfless resort. But a new hotel management group had taken over the property, and had engaged Devereux Emmet, a pioneer American golf course architect, to build a 6,500-yard course at Briarcliff. It would be ready for play in the coming spring.

Sarazen and Hutchison's West Coast tour began in San Francisco. After a week there, they moved down to Los Angeles. With the exception of one quick trip down to San Diego, they stayed in the LA area for almost a month, playing almost daily exhibition matches.

While Gene's days were full of golf, his nights were full as well. He played the area's nightlife circuit from the tips. He frequented the scene at the Coconut Grove, and he became a carousing pal of another young man who was hitting Hollywood in a big way—Howard Hughes. Gene became fodder for the tabloids of the day when he was seen on several occasions in the company of Pauline Garron, an up-and-coming young actress.

About halfway through his stay in Southern California, Gene's relationship with his new employer, the Briarcliff Lodge, began to turn sour. Apparently, his desire to play in the British Open and the amount of time it would require him to be away from Briarcliff never came up in their contract discussions. When it was brought to Briarcliff's attention, the resort was none too happy. Briarcliff was planning to showcase the new course in the spring and wanted its golf professional present, not in Scotland playing the British Open.

There were exchanges of telegrams back and forth, and a good bit of the disagreement was played out in the press. Gene told reporters that he was going to the British Open regardless. When told about Gene's statement, the management company executive at the Briarcliff huffed, "Well, we will just see about that!"

Sarazen and Hutchison departed Los Angeles late in February for Miami. On the way they made stops for events in Phoenix and San Antonio. In his exhibition match in Phoenix, Gene's caddie was a future U.S. senator and Republican candidate for president, Barry Goldwater.

A few weeks before reporting to his new post at the Briarcliff, Gene signed an endorsement deal with Wilson Sporting Goods. The company had decided to go into the golf market in a big way and wanted the game's hottest new star to represent their brand. The initial deal was for Gene to receive $6,000 a year plus an equal amount for travel expenses. The Wilson/Sarazen relationship would become the longest-running endorsement pact in professional sports, as Gene would remain under contract with Wilson until his death in 1999, a total of 75 years.

Gene's back and forth with Briarcliff over the British Open continued for 10 weeks. A few days after Gene formally started to work at Briarcliff, its board, feeling the heat from the sporting press and golf fans, voted to allow the reigning U.S. Open Champion, PGA Champion, and the Unofficial World Champion of Golf the time off he would need to play in the British Open.

Departing in early May with an abundance of fanfare, Sarazen traveled with Walter Hagen to the Open Championship aboard the ocean liner *Aquitania*. They arrived in England four and half weeks ahead of the British Open, which was to be held at Troon in Scotland.

Walter and Gene spent three weeks in England playing in a number of exhibitions and in two tournaments. In the first tournament, a match play event, they went head to head in the semifinals and Walter came out on top. He lost in the finals. In the second tournament, a medal play event, Gene put on a charge on the final day and won by two strokes.

Gene and Walter departed England and headed for Scotland a week and a half in advance of the Open Championship. This was the first time Troon was hosting the event. The Old Course at Troon was a classic seaside links layout with plenty of wind to contend with and deep rough interspersed with gorse and broom.

Of the 11 Americans who had made the trip over to Troon, Gene was by far the cockiest. He was not shy about boasting about his chances. Gene's bluster was viewed with wry smiles by the UK golf fans and press, as they were quick to point out that maturity was one of the key factors in their championship. Since 1920, the average age of the winners was 35.

The track record of young heralded American-bred golfers playing in their first Open Championship, to say the least, had been disappointing. In 1914, Frances Ouimet drew the largest gallery on opening day, as Great Britain's golf fans were anxious to see the young lad who had outdueled their greats, Harry Vardon and Ted Ray, in a play-off for the U.S. Open title at Brookline the year before. But by the end of the round, Ouimet had just a handful of followers. In perfect scoring conditions at Prestwick, the site of the first British Open in 1865, he had racked up a score of 86. At the tournament's end, he would claim 56th place, 26 strokes behind the winner, Harry Vardon.

As covered earlier, Walter Hagen had finished 52nd in his first Open Championship. In 1921, 21-year-old Bobby Jones made his first start in a British Open at the Old Course at St. Andrews. Jones was still a few years away from glory on the course as well as from his reputation as an even-dispositioned and unruffled Georgia gentleman. At this time, his short temper, foul mouth, and penchant for club throwing were talked about on par with his golf prowess.

Jones acquitted himself well on the first day of the tournament, but on day two the Old Course grabbed him. He started off badly and went downhill from there. By the time he reached the tee of the par-three 11th hole, the young Georgian had already expended 50 strokes. He bunkered his 51st shot. After strokes 52, 53, 54, and 55, Jones's ball was still in that same bunker. He lost it at that point and stormed off the course like a spoiled six-year-old, tearing his scorecard into small pieces along the way.

The best showing by a young American had been in the 1913 Open Championship, which was also held at St. Andrews. It was turned in by 1912 U.S. Open champion John McDermott. Just 19 at the time, McDermott finished in fifth place, a distant 11 strokes behind the winner.

The Open week's schedule called for 36 holes of qualifying. The qualifying would take place on Monday and Tuesday, with 18 holes being played each day. Wednesday was an off day. The Open would take place on Thursday and Friday with 36 holes being played each day. After practice rounds were concluded on Saturday, there would not be any golf played until the beginning of the qualifying rounds on Monday, as the Sabbath was strictly observed as a day of rest in Scotland.

On this Sunday, however, the peaceful calm of the Scots' Sabbath morning at Troon was broken by clanging sounds akin to those emanating from a boiler factory. The commotion was caused by nearly a dozen American golfers in the caddie house hammering and filing down the faces of their irons.

The reason they were engaged in this exercise was the result of an edict that had been issued early Saturday evening by the governing body of the British Open, the Royal and Ancient Golf Club of St. Andrews. The R&A's statement on the matter read in part:

> The rules committee has decided that clubs of corrugated, grooved, or
> slotted patterns constitute a substantial departure from the traditional

accepted forms and makes of golf clubs and accordingly are not permissible under the rules of the Royal and Ancient committee . . .
consequently they are not permissible in the Open Championship.

For some time, irons used by Americans had had small punch holes on
their faces. During practices rounds for the Open at Troon, the American
players had been putting an eye-popping amount of backspin on their
shots. This amazing amount of spin was due to a number of Americans
taking the punching of the faces of their irons to a whole new level. They
were making the punches much deeper. This raised the rim of each inden-
tion, roughing up the surface of the club face. This was the culprit for the
Americans' ability to take the amount of backspin that was being im-
parted on the ball to an all-time high, giving their shots greater distance
and bringing the balls to a stop quicker when they landed on the green.

In the opening salvos of the white-hot rivalry that would develop
between American golfers and those in Great Britain, whenever
Americans were victorious on British soil, the Brits believed they had
fallen victim, not to the skill of the American player, but to American
ingenuity. The British attitude in this regard began in the spring of 1904
at Royal St. George's Golf Club, located in the town of Sandwich, when
American Walter Travis claimed the British Amateur title.

Having won the 1900, 1901, and 1903 U.S. Amateurs titles, Travis, a
resident of Long Island, was considered the country's foremost golfer in
the early twentieth century. He did not take up golf until 1896, when he
was three months shy of his 35th birthday. Thin and slight in stature,
Travis played almost all of his rounds with a cigar in his mouth. His much
younger rivals called him "the Old Man."

In May 1904, Travis traveled to England to take a crack at the British
Amateur, a match play event. Thanks to a red-hot putter, Travis reached
the finals with relative ease. In that 36-hole final, he rolled over Edward
Blackwell, one of the longest hitters the British Empire had ever produced, by the count of four and three.

As expected, Blackwell outdrove Travis all day by 20 to 30 yards, but
Travis more than made up for his lack of distance with the same spectacu-
lar putting display he had exhibited in his previous four matches. Travis's
putter had a unique design, the likes of which the British had never seen.

The putter that Travis was using so superbly was a Schenectady Putter, named after its city of origin. It was the handiwork of a General

Electric engineer and avid golfer named Arthur F. "Frank" Knight, one of the top golfers at the Mohawk Golf Club in Schenectady, New York. Since the dawn of the game, the shaft of the putter had always been joined to its head on the near side of the club. Knight's Schenectady had the shaft joined to the center of the head of the putter.

Walter Travis was given a prototype of the Schenectady Putter just before it went to market, and he loved it. He used the Schenectady in winning the U.S. Amateur in 1903. As word spread that Travis was using a Schenectady, its sales soared.

Golf journalist and historian Bernard Darwin covered the British Amateur for the *Times* of London for over 40 years. He was the grandson of Charles Darwin, the famous naturalist whose theories on evolution decades earlier had created quite a stir in Great Britain and around the world.

Bernard had observed a key moment in the evolution of golf, as he was on hand for Travis's performance with his Schenectady at Royal St. George's. His account of Travis's performance was included in the book *A Round with Darwin: A Collection of the Golf Writings of Bernard Darwin*, an anthology of his golf writings published after his death in 1961:

> If it did not actually found the American golfing empire, it certainly gave the foundations of the British one a very definite shake. What I may call the Travis terror came on by degrees as he holed more long putts with his strange center-shafted putter, and, as our players went down before him one by one, we, who had at first esteemed his chances lightly, became more and more fatalistic. But this happened so gradually that I have in my mind's eye only one comprehensive picture of that small, vaguely sinister figure with the black cigar. He is standing still as a statue, Schenectady putter in hand, watching his ball rolling inexorably towards the hole.

Given he was the current holder of both the British Amateur and the U.S. Amateur titles, newspapers in the United Kingdom and the United States bestowed upon Travis the title of "World Champion of Golf." Travis received a hero's welcome when he returned to New York City, with a host of dinners and receptions given in his honor. His British Amateur trophy was put on display at one of the city's high-profile locations: Tiffany's, which at that time was located at Union Square.

In 1910, six years after Travis's victory, the R&A made a sweeping ruling barring a number of designs and styles of golf clubs. The R&A believed this move was warranted in order to protect the traditions and integrity of the game. On this list of banned clubs was the Schenectady Putter.

The relationship between the U.S. Golf Association and the R&A, the recognized governing body of the game, could best be described as amicable up to this point. Just two years prior, the Rules Committee of the R&A had sought input from the USGA on changes to the rules of the game. The USGA provided a list of over 20 recommendations, and many of these suggestions were incorporated into the rules changes the R&A adopted. So the banning of the Schenectady by the R&A, without any notice or input from the USGA, incensed a great many American golfers. Many of them were of the opinion that British golfers had been stewing about the role the Schenectady had played in Travis's British Amateur win in 1904, and that the R&A had had the putter in its cross-hairs ever since.

At the next annual meeting of the USGA, a resolution to disregard the R&A's banning of the Schenectady and to continue to allow its use in the United States was put forth. It won swift and overwhelming approval. It would be 41 years (1951) before the R&A would see fit to lift its ban on the Schenectady.

The next significant ruling the R&A would make was over what was then called ribbed (grooved) clubs. It would come in 1921, 11 years after the banning of the Schenectady. As with the punched clubs, the ribbed clubs were applying substantial backspin, and Americans in large numbers were using them. A month or so before the 1921 British Open, the R&A decreed that it was banning ribbed clubs. But unlike the immediate banning of punched clubs at Troon in 1923, this ruling would not go into effect until the 1922 British Open.

At the 1921 British Open at St. Andrews, when the native of St. Andrews turned American citizen, Jock Hutchison, showed up to compete, he had ribbed clubs in his bag—extremely ribbed clubs. Hutchison's play with his irons during that week was as strong as anyone had ever seen at the Old Course. As detailed earlier, he made a hole-in-one on the first day. He ended up tied at the end of regulation play with one of the Crown's top amateurs, Roger Wethered. Jock went on to defeat him in a 36-hole play-off by nine strokes, thanks to a wealth of dandy approach shots. Many of the British faithful believed that Hutchison's clubs had been the reason he won. One British sportswriter described the outcome as a "victory by implement, not by man."

The day after the R&A's ruling at Troon, Hagen, despite the fact he was fuming, decided to appear nonchalant about the ban. All the other Americans except one joined Hagen in not commenting on the matter. The exception was Sarazen, who gave the press an earful, highlighted by this comment that was carried in the *Washington Post*: "All the R&A did by making this ruling was to get themselves in bad. I probably would not make another trip over here."

In the first day of qualifying, Gene displayed no ill effects from having to switch to smooth-faced clubs. Among the 222 players that teed off that day, Gene was the low American and stood in 10th place overall. Most of the other Americans were off their games, especially Walter Hagen, who stood in 164th place. With only the low 80 qualifying, Walter's odds on making the field appeared to be extra-long. On the other hand, one would have thought Gene was a virtual shoo-in, but that would prove not to be the case.

Since arriving in Troon, Gene had let it be known that he was not concerned about the challenges the elements could present at a seaside course. In today's jargon, Gene in fact doubled down on the matter. He let it be known that he was praying for wind and rain. He maintained that nobody would be able to beat him in those conditions.

Due to the large field, qualifying was taking place at two courses: the Open venue at Troon, and a municipal course. Gene had drawn the municipal course for the first day. He had a late starting time, and the weather had been ideal. For day two, he would be on the course that would host the Open Championship, a much tougher tract. Gene also had an early starting time, which would be a huge negative on this particular day because the wind and rain he had been praying for showed up, and showed up with a vengeance.

On the second hole, as he walked to his drive, Gene's umbrella was blown out of his hand. The umbrella must have taken his game with it. He took an eight on that hole. From that point, his tee shots were rough bound, his approaches bunkered. Makeable putts that would have saved par were woefully off target. He went out in seven over par and came home an additional six over par for an 85. To make matters worse, those teeing off later in the day had a much easier time because the weather improved dramatically. When it was all said and done, Gene missed making the field by one stroke.

Four other Americans joined Gene in not making the field. Six did, with three of them slipping into the field by just one stroke. Included in that trio was Hagen. He was assisted by a late starting time. Also, he was playing the easier municipal course and improved his first day score at Troon by 11 shots.

During the off-day between qualifying and the first 36 holes of the Open Championship, Gene packed his bags and went into exile at the Gleneagles golf resort in central Scotland until the championship was over.

In the championship, Hagen, who made the field by one stroke, missed forcing a play-off for the title by one stroke. The winner was Arthur Havers, a 25-year-old English professional from Norwich, Scotland. Hagen's downfall in the final round was his putting. He had a half-dozen putts come up short or just slide by the hole. The worst of the latter came at the 10th hole, when he missed from 12 inches.

Shortly before they boarded their ship for home, Hagen and Sarazen commented on the club-banning edict during an interview with a reporter for the *Sunday Times*. Those comments were carried in the paper's next edition. For Walter, these were his first comments to the press on the matter. He said, "It was unsportsmanlike the way the clubs were banned at the 11th hour." Gene added, "It was a great mistake to have men at St. Andrews with such autocratic power."

Gene and Walter's arrival back in New York City was a far cry from the throng that had greeted Walter's return with the Claret Jug the year before—just a few well-wishers and a couple of reporters. After Gene's disheartening showing at Troon, he undoubtedly wanted to lay low until the U.S. Open, which was going to take place at the Inwood Country Club on Long Island in four weeks. Keeping a low profile, however, was not in the cards. He was seen by thousands each day. A film he had shot while in Los Angeles over the winter was now being shown in theaters in the New York City area. It was a short reel that ran before the main feature. Its title was *Golf as Played by Gene Sarazen* and it featured, for its time, innovative slow motion that broke down Gene's swing in its various stages. One reviewer called it the most interesting film of its kind ever produced.

Three hundred and sixty golfers signed up for the Open at Inwood. Although strong in numbers, the field lacked an international flair, as there were no notable entries from abroad. The two entries that were getting the most attention were Gene and Bobby Jones. The buzz about Gene was which Gene was going to show up, the defending champion or the one who couldn't make the field at the British Open.

For Bobby Jones, who was considered to have the finest golf swing in the world, the question was whether he had developed the composure to win a major tournament. His record in three previous U.S. Opens was an eighth-place finish, a fifth-place finish, and a second-place finish respectively. He also had a second-place finish in the U.S. Amateur tournament.

With a field of 360, qualifying had to be spread over a four-day period. Each day a quarter of the entries would play 36 holes, with the low 18 and ties earning a spot in the field. Gene drew a spot in the first day's qualifier. Inwood Country Club is situated on a peninsula in Jamaica Bay. It has the feel of a Scottish links course, with wind conditions often being a significant factor. As he teed off in his qualifier, Gene had to be having a flashback, as he was facing gale-like winds that were every bit as formidable as those that produced his debacle at Troon. The scoring conditions were so bad, that at the end of the day, only 57 of the 90 players that started bothered to turn in a scorecard. Gene was one of that 57; in fact he was the lowest qualifier, with a score of four over par.

Walter Hagen and Bobby Jones qualified for the field on the fourth day, with scores that put them in the middle of the pack of that day's top 18.

On the first day of the Open, weather was not a factor and, it turned out, neither was Gene. During the morning round, he shot seven over par. In the afternoon round he was six over and, for all intents and purposes, a playing spectator for the remaining 36 holes. Bobby Jones, on the other hand, was a big factor. Jones was paired with Walter Hagen. It was Friday the 13th and the Jones/Hagen twosome had been the 13th pairing to go off the first tee. But there was nothing unlucky about those circumstances, at least in Jones's case. He shot a one-under-par 71 in the morning and a one-over 73 in the afternoon. His 36-hole total of 144 left him just two strokes behind leader Jock Hutchison. Hagen struggled and joined Sarazen way back in the pack.

On the final day, Sarazen was paired with Jones. The wind became a factor early in the day and scores shot up. When the tallying was done for round three, it was essentially a two-horse race between Jones and a long-shot pro out of New Jersey, Bobby Cruickshank, who held a two-shot lead. Cruickshank was an undersized Scottish transplant, who during World War I had pulled off an endeavor with very long odds indeed: an escape from a German prison camp.

In the final round Jones and Sarazen went off a number of groups ahead of Cruickshank. As the round progressed, the lead moved back and forth between Jones and Cruickshank but down the stretch, Jones pulled away. At the 18th tee, he had a three-stroke advantage.

Covering 425 yards and with the green protected in front by a small pond, given the performance characteristics of ball and clubs at that time, the par-four 18th at Inwood was a solid test. Jones's approach shot to the 18th missed the green by a wide margin to the right and landed in the gallery. It took several minutes for security to clear the gallery so Jones could play his shot. Jones had held his temper in check all week, but this delay got to him. He was clearly angry. When he finally played the shot, he dribbled his ball into a bunker that lay between himself and the green. It took three more shots for him to get his ball into the cup for a double-bogey six.

Despite that poor finish, it appeared that Jones would still win by one, and the crowd rushed around him as he exited the green. Sarazen, who had been on the receiving end of this kind of overwhelming outpouring of adoration a year earlier at Skokie, was brushed aside in the rush.

As it would turn out, the celebration over Jones at the 18th green was some 24 hours premature. Cruickshank hit the approach shot of his career at the 18th. It checked up just four feet from the cup and then he rolled in his birdie putt. His three and Jones's six at the home hole left them tied at the end of regulation, setting up an 18-hole play-off the next day.

Given the fact that Jones had butchered the 72nd hole, while Cruick-shank had made a monumental birdie to knot things up, it was the general opinion that Jones would have a tough time recovering in the play-off from that final hole collapse. But that proved to be anything but the case. When the playoff reached the 18th tee, they were tied. Cruickshank's drive there was abysmal. He topped it and it traveled just 100 yards and stopped out of the fairway behind a clump of trees. Jones's drive was respectable in distance but it came to rest some six feet out of the fairway on trampled-down parched grass.

Cruickshank had no choice but to lay up short of the pond and try and get up and down. Jones, on the other hand, had a choice to make: to lay up as well and enter into a pitching and putting contest with his rival or, despite the bad lie and the pond, go for the green. He chose the latter.

Jones grabbed a mid-iron and wasted little time in executing the shot. Reporters some distance away thought Jones was taking a smooth practice swing until they heard the roar from the crowd at the green when the shot landed and rolled up to within six feet of the hole. Those standing close to Jones said the ball was tracking for the flag its entire flight. Cruickshank misplayed his third into a bunker by the green and took three more shots to get down for a six. Jones two-putted to claim his first major victory. The Bobby Jones era had begun. His approach shot in the play-off would be called "the shot heard 'round the world." It would keep that distinction until Sarazen's 4-wood swing at Jones's course in Augusta some 12 years later.

5

THE BALL WITH
SPAGHETTI SAUCE ON IT

There were two big golf events left on the 1923 golf calendar. For Bobby Jones and the rest of the countries' elite amateurs, there was the U.S. Amateur that would be held at the Floosmoor Country Club outside Chicago, and for the professionals, the PGA Championship near New York City at the Pelham Country Club in Westchester County.

In terms of stature at this time, the U.S. Amateur was perhaps slipping just a bit from being equal to the U.S. Open but would sustain its current position for most of the next decade thanks to Bobby Jones. Bobby didn't fare well at Floosmoor in 1923—he was eliminated by the eventual winner, Max R. Marston, in the third round. But he would win the event in 1924, 1925, 1927, 1929, and 1930.

By contrast, the PGA Championship, born in 1916 and postponed because of World War I in 1917 and 1918, had been struggling to develop its credibility as one of golf's major tournaments. The event at Pelham, however, would give this championship a huge shot in the arm, as it produced the best marquee match possible in its final match, Sarazen versus Hagen.

Walter Hagen breezed through his bracket and then destroyed his opponent in the semifinals 12-up, with 11 to play.

Gene Sarazen skated to victory in his first two matches, the first by a count of 8-up with 7 to go and in the second by a tally of 11-up with 10 to go. In his third match, he faced off against Alec Campbell. Although he was pushing 50 years, Campbell, a Scottish transplant, was no pushover, having recorded five top-10 finishes in U.S. Open play. He held up against Sarazen deep into the match before finally being closed out at the 33rd hole three and two.

In his next match, Sarazen went up against a two-time winner of the PGA Championship and the winner of 1921 U.S. Open, Jim Barnes, for a spot in the final four. Barnes, as mentioned earlier, was a transplant form England. He stood six feet, four inches tall, and had a highly polished game but an abrasive personality. Barnes knew the Pelham Country Club course like the back of his hand. He was its head professional.

The Barnes/Sarazen match-up had a special feel about it because of an attitude both men shared: an extreme disdain for each other. This mutually shared contempt had its origin at the 1922 Southern Open in New Orleans. The two were paired in one of the rounds. On that occasion, Jim was not having a particularly good day and Gene made a comment meant to provide some solace to his playing companion. Jim, in a bristling tone, essentially told Gene what he could do with his comment.

Their relationship moved into the irreconcilable category a few months later at the U.S. Open at Skokie. It was a day or two before qualifying, and Sarazen was looking for someone to go out with him for a practice round. He ran into Frances Ouimet and asked the 1913 U.S. Open champion if he could join him. Ouimet said it would be okay with him, but he would have to check with the other two players he had already lined up for the round: Chick Evans, who had won the 1916 U.S. Open and the 1916 U.S. Amateur, and Barnes. They encountered Evans and Barnes a few moments later. Evans said it would be fine if Gene joined them, but Barnes said no.

In their match at Pelham, Gene grabbed the lead at the first hole. As the match stretched out, Gene kept adding to his lead. At the tee of their 30th hole, Gene had his foot on the back of Jim's neck. He was four-up with just seven holes remaining. In match play, however, momentum can turn on a dime. On that hole, Gene misplayed his approach and could not get up and down, and Jim shaved the lead to three. On the next hole, Gene lost it when he hit his approach shot out of bounds. They halved the next hole. On the 33rd hole, both were on the green in regulation. Jim was 15 feet from the cup, while Gene was only 10. Jim drained his putt; Gene missed and his advantage was down to just one. They halved the 34th hole. The next hole was a long par five and Jim really turned it on. He reached the green in two and then won the hole when he dropped a 40-foot eagle putt to square the match.

The par-four 18th at Pelham was just over 300 yards. Jim, with the honor, went for the green. He was off line and ended up short of the green in a tough lie. Gene went for the green as well. His ball made it and came to rest just 15 feet from the pin. Jim was too strong with his pitch and skirted past the pin into the back fringe. He almost holed his chip for birdie as it stopped just three inches from the hole. Gene had two putts to win. His first effort came up uncomfortably short, leaving him a knee-knocker to take the match. As was his norm on putts of this length he wasted little time in executing it, rolling it into the cup to finish off Jim Barnes.

In his semifinal match, Gene faced off against the runner-up in that year's U.S. Open, Bobby Cruickshank, and had an easy time, taking a seven-up with five to play decision.

The Hagen/Sarazen final was a spectator's delight. It had it all—excellent shots, a brouhaha, a little mystery, and great drama. The support in the gallery was almost equally divided. In their autobiographies, written 25-plus years later, both Gene and Walter had vivid recollections about the gallery that day. Sarazen recalled it this way: "The final of the PGA between Walter and myself might not have taken on the proportions of a grudge match, which it did, if our supporters hadn't been clawing at each other. . . Hagen's followers were an arrogant bunch." Hagen wrote this about the gallery: "I'll say right here that Pelham was thickly populated with enthusiastic Italians, they were all eager for their little compatriot to win."

The morning round was far from a demonstration of stellar golf. It ended with the match all square. Each player had finished at three over par. What pushed the scores to this level was the duo's putting. There was only a one-putt green between them.

Despite their overall lackluster play, there were some fireworks at the sixth hole. Gene's approach shot lay between two bunkers and a foot path. There were some leaves in front of his ball and he asked the match's referee, who was standing near the flagstick, if he could move the leaves. There was no reply. He asked again and the referee nodded his head in the affirmative. As soon as Gene started to move the leaves, Walter, who was positioned near his ball on the far side of green and had not been paying attention to the goings-on between Gene and the official, charged over. In a blustery tone, he asked, "Hey, what's going on here? You know that's illegal. . . . How about playing by the rules?"

It turned out that Hagen had not been the only person involved in the match who was not paying attention. When Walter protested, the official concurred with him. A shocked Gene got his back up as well and yelled back to the official that he had asked before moving the leaves and that the official had indicated that he could. Gene then asked, "What do you want me to do now!" There were a few moments of tense silence, and then the official responded with, "Go ahead and play your ball."

Still fuming at Walter's remarks, Gene stubbed his chip far short of the cup and missed the putt, giving the hole to Walter. On the way to the next tee he told Walter he was glad that he lost the hole so there would be nothing to squawk about later.

Although it is not mentioned in the numerous press accounts used to chronicle this match, Hagen contended in his autobiography, *The Walter Hagen Story*, that he was the victim of another "squawkable" incident later during the first 18. This one involved interference by a spectator that almost assuredly saved Sarazen from losing a hole. It happened on the par-four 14th. According to Hagen, Sarazen's approach shot was headed into the water hazard that fronted the green when a young lad in a red sweater bolted out of the gallery and stopped the ball with his foot. The hole ended up being halved.

Their match remained square through the first 4 holes of the afternoon 18. Then Gene's putter heated up. He dropped a 30-foot birdie for a win at five and a12-footer for a win at six. Hagen appeared poised to turn the tide at seven, when he dropped his approach shot down in birdie range. But he missed his birdie putt and then missed his par attempt. Gene parred and was now fully in command with a three-up lead.

Hagen cut the lead to two-up with a birdie at 11. The next four holes were halved with par-birdie-par-par with two of what would have been hole-winning putts by Hagen lipping out. At the short par-three 16th, both were on the green but Sarazen's putter turned on him. He three-putted, and his lead was down to one.

At the par-five 17th, Gene and Walter both hit strong drives and both opted to go for the green in two. Gene, away, went first and deposited his shot in a greenside bunker. Walter followed, and a death groan came up from his supporters in the gallery as his ball sailed out of bounds. It looked like their man was done, but Walter did not appear to be fazed.

After all, he was the game's king when it came to recovery shots. He took a drop at the spot where he had hit his last shot and fired off his fairway wood again. This ball's flight was the total opposite of the wayward out-of-bounds shot; it was on a direct line with the flag. It did land short, but had plenty of roll. It bisected the two bunkers that guarded the front of the green. When it had rolled out it was resting just 20 feet from the cup.

Sand play at this time was far from Gene's strong suit. His explosion shot left more than a little to be desired. It checked up some 30 feet from the hole. Gene's putt for a birdie that would have ended the match was aggressive—too aggressive, as it sped by the hole some six feet. Walter took his time studying his line and then smoothly stroked his putt. To his followers in the crowd it looked good from the start and it was, falling into the hole at the perfect pace for a remarkable par. Gene had to be feeling the pressure from the sudden turn of events. His attempt for par slid by and with his bogey, the match was now all square.

At the drivable par-four 18th, both Walter and Gene tried to make the green with their tee shots. Walter's drive didn't make it. It landed in a greenside bunker. Gene's drive did make it, but it was some distance from the hole. Walter's play from the sand left him a makeable putt for birdie. Gene's eagle attempt was too strong, and it went by the hole some six feet. Walter's birdie attempt also was too strong, but it turned out to be a great putt. His ball stopped almost directly in line with Gene's ball for what was called a "stymie." Under the rules of golf at that time, Hagen did not have to mark his ball. It was up to Gene to chip his ball over his, or try and putt around it. Gene tried the latter and missed, and for the first time in the PGA Championship's history, the event went to extra holes.

The play-off began at the first hole, a long par four. Both hit fine approaches. Walter was away and he rolled in his putt for birdie. Gene's putt from about seven feet for birdie and a half looked to be just a tad off in pace. It hung on the lip. Walter looked at Gene, expecting him to begin walking over to congratulate him, but then gravity interceded on Gene's behalf. His ball slowly toppled into the hole.

The second hole was a short dogleg par four. It was drivable but the players had to cut the dogleg on the left, carrying the ball over trees and a row of small houses. Gene decided to go for the green, but he didn't quite get all of it, and it was a little more to the left than it needed to be. His ball disappeared from sight and could be heard rattling off a house that was well out of bounds. Gene played a provisional. Walter played it safe with his drive.

Walking to his drive, Walter had to be thinking he had it won. Then he heard a euphoric shout. Gene's caddie had found his first ball—in bounds!

Given the ball's original flight path and where Gene's caddie was now standing, Walter did not see any possible way that it could be Gene's ball. He double-timed over to Gene's ball to conduct his own inspection. Gene was playing a red-lettered Wilson ball. Walter gazed down at it and then remarked to Gene that it had to be his ball because "it's got spaghetti sauce on it," referring to the red "Wilson" lettering and Gene's ethnicity. Gene was irked by Walter's dig at his Italian lineage, and settled the score for that remark with his next shot.

In later accounts by both players, each had a different view as to the condition of Sarazen's lie. Hagen contended it was practically teed up. Sarazen said it was resting in a tough lie of heavy rough. What is undisputable is that Sarazen executed an excellent shot from the ball's location. Although only 40 yards from the hole, the pin was tucked behind a bunker. Sarazen's shot carried the bunker and then curled up just two feet from the hole.

Hagen was faced with a pitch of even less distance. But the turn of events in the last few minutes obviously was enough to rattle even Hagen. He chunked his pitch into the bunker. He wasn't quite done, however; he caused Sarazen and those in his camp a moment or two of great angst when his explosion shot from the bunker almost found the bottom of the cup. Sarazen conceded Hagen's par and then rolled in his birdie to retain his PGA champion title.

During the afternoon round of the Hagen/Sarazen match at Pelham, the gallery at the 10th green was joined by a man who had just walked three miles from his home to get there. The man did not stay for long. He watched Gene miss a long putt, then did an about-face and headed back to his residence. The man's name was Frederico Saraceni. He was Gene's father.

A native-born Italian, Frederico Saraceni was a carpenter by trade. It was far from the profession he had hoped to have. He wanted to be a priest and was well along in his studies, but before he could finish, Frederico lost both parents in a short period of time and, due to the financial hardship this created, had to discontinue that pursuit.

At the monastery where he had been studying, one of the tasks he was assigned was building wooden caskets. This led him to choose carpentry as a means to make a living. Times were hard in Italy. Shortly after he married Gene's mother, Adela, a relative who had moved to the United States sent word that there was a construction boom taking place in America, and that a good carpenter could do very well. Soon Frederico and his wife were part of the huge Italian immigration to the United States. Once in America, their family expanded. Gene's sister, Margaret, came first, and Gene was born two years later.

Frederico was an excellent carpenter, but he struggled with the business side of his trade. His command of the Italian language was at the scholarly level, but he never fully embraced the English language. This affected him negatively in his business dealings; it led to misunderstandings and others easily took advantage of him.

On most evenings, after putting in what was typically a 12-hour day, Frederico would retreat to the cellar of his home where he had set up a small area with a lamp and a comfortable chair. He would stay there until the early morning hours, smoking his pipe and reading the classics in Italian.

Gene began making a contribution to the family's finances at a very young age, selling the *Saturday Evening Post* at a railroad station near their home. When he was 10, he began to caddie with his father's blessing, as it provided a small but steady stream of income. The game at that time was by and large considered to be a vice of the well-to-do, but that image was beginning to change, especially for the multitude of young boys in the caddie yard. This change was due to John McDermott, who in 1911 became the youngest player to win the U.S. Open, at age 19. McDermott wasn't some rich kid. He was one of their own, who had graduated from the caddie yard just a few years before his big win. Thanks to him, caddying was no longer just a source of income; it was also a possible path to glory. This feeling would swell the following year, when McDermott repeated as U.S. Open champion, and then went through the roof in 1913 when former caddie Francis Ouimet defeated the British greats at Brookline.

The caddie winning streak continued in the 1914 Open, when Walter Hagen, late of the caddie yard at the Rochester Country Club, took first. One stroke behind him was the pride of the Chicago caddie circuit, Chick Evans.

The dreams of glory in the caddie yard were cooled down in 1915 when a home-bred golfer with a country-club pedigree, Jerome Travers, took the crown, but these dreams were reignited to full flame when Chick Evans won both the U.S. Open and the U.S. Amateur in 1916.

After Evans's wins, the rush to the caddie yard turned into a stampede. On any Saturday morning across the country there was an endless line of young boys, each waiting to be assigned a bag to carry.

From the time he first began caddying Gene had always worked hard on his game. The great success of the caddie yard graduates fueled him to work even harder, with a career in golf as his goal. Hard times, however, soon sidelined his golfing ambitions. To bring in more money for the family, his father pulled him off the course to work as his helper. Soon after that, the United States entered World War I, and the two worked together building barracks at an Army training station.

That job lasted three months, and Gene put in some very long hours hammering nail after nail. Soon after that job ended, Frederico took a job at a plant in Bridgewater, Connecticut, that was producing artillery components for the war effort, and the family relocated. Gene found work there at a small arms manufacturer. As fate would have it, the job, in a less-than-ideal way, would provide him a ticket back to the golf course.

One day Gene came down with a cold and for the next several weeks, he just couldn't seem to shake it. Then it began to get worse. A few days later, he was in the hospital being treated for pneumonia. Severe complications developed. It was touch and go for several days. Surgery was required to extract the fluid that had built up in his lungs. After the surgery, Gene slowly began the road to recovery. Fearing Gene might now have chronic issues with his respiratory system, his doctor advised him to avoid the confined and dusty space of a factory and to work outdoors.

It was a lengthy recovery period. During that time, Gene told his parents that he was returning to golf and would pursue it as a career. Frederico was opposed to it. Gene's mother, Adela, supported her son. There were some tense times at the dinner table during his recovery period. With Frederico often implying that Gene looked healthy enough to work in almost any endeavor, Gene would counter with his doctor's recommendations.

According to Gene in his book, *Thirty Years of Championship Golf,* the missed putt at the 10th green at Pelham was the only shot his father ever witnessed him take. One would have thought that Frederico would have been his son's biggest fan at that point. By pursing his passion, Gene had achieved phenomenal success at a very young age. And he had shared that success with his parents. Frederico was in the Pelham area because after his wins at the U.S. Open and PGA, Gene had purchased a nice home for his parents there.

The win at the PGA restored Gene's confidence in his game. He announced that he was putting his tremendous failure at Troon and his hostility toward the R&A over their club banning behind him. He would return to England next year to compete in the British Open. It would turn out that the trip across the Atlantic would also have another purpose—it would serve as a honeymoon.

In an interview after he won the U.S. Open at Skokie, Gene was asked if he was married. Gene answered, "Goodness no, but bring on the girls and be sure to tell them I am single." Soon after that, Gene was the consummate high-profile bachelor. He soaked up the nightlife in New York City, and later in Hollywood during his swing out west.

As mentioned earlier, while in Hollywood Gene had been seen in the company of up-and-coming actress Pauline Garron. In early December 1923, *Time* magazine reported that Gene and Pauline were engaged. A few days after the magazine hit the street, Garron issued a statement from the set of a movie she was shooting, stating that reports of the engagement were false. How this story made the press is anybody's guess, since Gene had not been on the West Coast in almost a year. But it turns out the story of Gene Sarazen's engagement was only a few months premature.

In the winter of 1923, Gene had gone to Miami following his lengthy stay on the West Coast. He stayed there several weeks before returning to Hollywood to shoot the short feature film on his golf. While in Miami he met a young lady, a pretty blonde named Mary Henry, just 16 and still in high school. They had several dates before he departed. The two stayed in touch via letters during the spring and summer of 1923.

Soon after his win at Pelham, Gene returned to the Miami area for the winter and the couple's relationship took off. Before Gene departed Miami that spring to resume his duties at Briarcliff Lodge, he proposed. The date for their wedding was set for early June.

6

A HONEYMOON AT THE OPEN CHAMPIONSHIP

The USGA made two big changes for the 1924 U.S. Open. The association was moving the event forward on the calendar to a position ahead of the British Open—it was set for the first week in June at Walter Hagen's old club, the Oakland Hills Country Club in Birmingham, Michigan—and for the first time, there would be sectional qualifying. The qualifying would take place at two sites. For golfers residing in the East, their qualifier would be at the Worcester Country Club in Worcester, Massachusetts, and for golfers in the West, qualifying would take place at the Oak Park Country Club in Chicago. Each qualifier would have approximately 160 entrants, with the top 40 and ties advancing.

The date for Mary Henry and Gene Sarazen's wedding was set for June 10th. This was three days after the conclusion of the U.S. Open, and one day before the couple would sail for what would be a working honeymoon for Gene, the British Open at the Royal Liverpool Golf Club in Hoylake, England.

Gene, along with Walter Hagen, qualified at Worcester but neither was at the top of their game. Both were in the bottom third of qualifiers. After Worcester, Gene headed back home to obtain a marriage license. He left the next day for Oakland Hills.

At the U.S. Open, Gene remained off his game. After the first 36 holes on day one, he was six strokes off the pace. He finished the final day 16 strokes behind the winner, Cyril Walker. Born in England, Walker had immigrated to the United States in 1914. He would later become one of the game's most tragic stories, falling victim to alcoholism and drinking himself first out of big-time competition, and then into a downward spiral that would lead to rock bottom. Walker would later have to resort to working as a caddie and a dishwasher. He ended up homeless. Shortly after being granted shelter in a Hackensack, New Jersey, jail in August 1948, some 24 years after his U.S. Open win, Walker died of pneumonia.

Bobby Jones finished in second place at Oakland Hills, three strokes behind Walker. Hagen finished in a tie for fourth.

Gene and Mary's wedding took place on a Tuesday at the Briarcliff Lodge. It was a small but classy affair. In Mary, Gene had found the ideal spouse. She was intelligent and very poised, which helped him overcome the inadequacies he harbored over his lack of education. Through the good times and the bad, her support of his career was unwavering. Mary learned to speak Italian so that she could communicate easily with Gene's parents, and she delved into Italian cooking in a big way. Their union would last until Mary's death, 62 years later in 1986.

The couple spent their first night at the Briarcliff and then sailed for England. Accompanying them on board were Hagen and Edna, Hagen's second wife. They had been married the previous spring.

Based on his failure to qualify at Troon, Great Britain's oddsmakers were listing Sarazen as a long shot in their Open Championship at 30 to 1. The favorite was the winner from the year before, Arthur Havers, at four to one. Hagen rated an eight to one shot.

In the two weeks they had to prepare for the event, Sarazen worked hard to ensure he would be able to clean up the doubts the British had about his game. Hagen was also working to do some cleaning up—not on his game, but in the public relations realm. In addition to his ranting about the banning by the R&A of punched clubs at the 1923 British Open, Hagen had been quoted in the press as believing that British golf professionals were lazy when it came to working on their games, and he was receiving a good deal of flak about it. He was letting anyone that would listen know he had been misquoted. What he had said was that British golf professionals seemed lazy. He attributed this to the way they were treated by the membership at the clubs where they were employed. In the States, a pro spends a considerable amount of time playing his home course with its members, at their request. This was in stark contrast to Great Britain, where pros were seldom invited to play with a member.

Hagen declared that he actually said this: "If a British professional seems lazy about practicing, it's because he must take his rounds alone."

The first day of qualifying at Royal Liverpool for Gene was a repeat of what had occurred the year before at Troon. He appeared to be almost assured a spot, as he finished in the top ten. Walter Hagen, on the other hand, was again in danger of not making the field. Whereas weather had played a huge factor in Gene's debacle in failing to qualify at Troon, it was not a factor in day two at Royal Liverpool. The weather was ideal, and Gene's second round easily placed him in the field.

For Walter, just as it had been at Troon where he slipped into the field by one stroke, his making the field at Royal Liverpool was a real nail-biter. In fact, he was almost disqualified before he teed off. His train to the course had been delayed, and he was 10 minutes late for his tee time. At first officials were going to disqualify him, but he appealed his case. The officials huddled together for several minutes in deliberation before finally ruling in his favor.

Once on the course, Walter turned in a stellar round and made the field. Instead of making it by one stroke as he did the year before, he improved by 100 percent, making the field this time by two strokes—and it was a two on a hole that was the difference. This very important deuce came not on a par three but on a par four.

Gene never got on track in his first Open Championship. After the first 36 holes on day one, he was in the middle of the pack in the 80-player field, thanks in large part to his three-putting eight greens. For the final 36 holes on day two, it was more of the same. He finished in 41st place.

Walter, on the other hand, was in a tie for third just two strokes back after day one. Shortly after concluding his play that day, he visited a local gambling hall and put down $250 on himself to win the event. It proved to be a very wise move.

After the morning round on the final day, two golfers had pulled away from the field and were tied for the lead. They were Hagen and Ernie Whitcomb, a British professional. Whitcomb went out ahead of Hagen. Midway through his back nine, Hagen received word that Whitcomb was in the clubhouse and stood one stroke behind him. Hagen lost opportunities to expand his lead coming in, and after reaching the par-five 15th in two, he three-putted. His birdie attempt at 17 was too strong and popped out of the hole.

Things got really interesting at the 18th green when Hagen was too strong with his approach, which left him a long downhill putt from the back edge of the green. He was tentative with his first putt, leaving it short by six feet. His putt for par and the victory was a double-breaker. Hagen gave it great deal of study and executed a perfect roll. As his ball took the last break and headed for the center of the cup, he threw his putter into the air, never to see it again.

Edna Hagen rushed onto the green to embrace her husband, beating the rush of other spectators by a scant second. Both Edna and Walter were hoisted onto the shoulders of crowd members and carried into the Royal Liverpool Clubhouse. Edna's entry marked the first time a female had been allowed to darken the clubhouse doors and enter its hallowed halls.

On their trip across the Atlantic, the Hagens and the Sarazens had decided to add the French Open to their schedule. It took place ten days after the British Open at the La Boulie Golf Club just outside Paris. After the first day, it looked as though Gene would also have a good chance of joining Walter in bringing back an Open title to the United States. He was the leader after the first day's 36 holes.

A few hours after the conclusion of the last two rounds on the final day, the scores were cabled to the Associated Press's headquarters in New York City. The sports editor looked at Gene's score for the third round and thought it was unbelievably high. Thinking it was a mistake, he cabled back to France and requested they check Sarazen's score. A short while later the score was confirmed. It was an 88.

Gene started that round off on a very sour note at the first hole. He played a poor drive that left a tall tree between his ball and the green. A member of the gallery asked Gene how he was going to play the shot. His reply was that he was going to hook his ball around the tree—and he did, but it took three attempts to pull it off. His first two attempts started right and stayed right, and both sailed out of bounds. He ended up with a nine on the hole. Over the remaining 17 holes, Gene's score card was peppered with bogeys and double-bogeys, and he finished the third round 16 over par.

Three months later, Gene went for his third consecutive win at the PGA Championship at the French Lick Springs Golf Club in French Lick, Indiana. Gene won his first match, which pushed his string of undefeated matches in the event to 13. The string was ended the next day, when he fell to Larry Nabholtz, an unheralded pro from Ohio, two and one. Walter Hagen was the victor at French Lick, beginning a string of what would be four straight PGA Championships.

Although Gene's performance in 1924 left him out of the headlines, he had a namesake that was making plenty of them. Like Gene in 1922, this Sarazen had seemingly come out of nowhere. He was a lot taller that Gene, he had four legs, and he wasn't classified as a home-bred. He was a thoroughbred.

Mrs. W. K. Vanderbilt, the former Virginia Fair, was the heiress to a Nevada silver mining operation that made millions. In 1899, she married into one of the richest families in America—the Vanderbilts, whose wealth had come from the railroad and shipping industries. In the early 1920s, Mrs. Vanderbilt, nicknamed Birdie, established her own racing stable. She purchased the then two-year-old Sarazen from his original owner after he had won three races. At fifteen hands tall, Sarazen was short by thoroughbred standards. He had a difficult temperament that made him hard to handle. To take some of the edge off his temperament, his original owner had him gelded.

Sarazen was a favorite to win the 1924 Kentucky Derby, but he had to be scratched from the field because of an illness. He made a full recovery and went on to complete the 1924 racing season undefeated, capturing all 10 races he entered. This earned him the award as the Horse of the Year.

Although Gene's performance in 1924 was lackluster, he did produce what was most likely the biggest roar of the year on a golf course. This happened in late October at the Briarcliff Lodge course at about 8:00 p.m. Briarcliff was hosting the convention of the Illuminating Engineers Society. Most of the first fairway was illuminated, and for two nights Gene demonstrated his golf game for those in attendance.

By the second night newspaper coverage, word of mouth, and the huge spotlight that was also being demonstrated drew a multitude of curious onlookers. Press accounts put the number of those in attendance at 10,000. That evening, Gene generated a tumultuous roar when he fired off a shot from approximately 200 yards that landed a few feet short of the pin and then disappeared into the hole.

Holing that shot under the lights was Gene's swan song for his employment at Briarcliff. He had signed on for the coming year at the Fresh Meadow Country Club in Flushing, New York. Fresh Meadow had opened with much fanfare in September 1923. It was designed by A. W.

Tillinghast, the designer of such famed layouts as Baltusrol, Wing Foot, and Bethpage Black. Fresh Meadow was on par with those designs as a superb test of golf.

Gene and Mary spent the winter in the Miami area and returned to New York City in early March for Gene to assume his duties at Fresh Meadow. Gene would be working out of the club's second clubhouse. Its first had burned down nine days after the club first opened.

Back in 1917, after his bout with pneumonia and his decision to pursue golf as a career, Gene needed a place to work his game back into shape. But he was in a tough spot when it came to having a place to practice, because he had zero funds. To further complicate the situation, he was now residing in Connecticut but all of his golfing contacts were back in New York City and northern New Jersey. But fate shined upon him, and he caught a break he would never forget.

Gene approached the pro at a local nine-hole public course, Al Ciuci, and explained his situation. Ciuci graciously allowed Gene to practice on the course at non-peak hours as long as he stayed out of the way of the paying customers. Over the ensuing months, Ciuci took a keen interest in Gene and his game, and helped Gene get his first interview with George Sparling at the Brooklawn Golf Club. At Fresh Meadow, Gene was allowed to select who would be his assistant pro—he chose Al Ciuci. Gene would stay at Fresh Meadows for six years. Ciuci would stay a little longer; his tenure would last 37 years. He would succeed Gene as head professional and would remain in the club's employ until his retirement in 1972.

As it had been the year before, the first major event of 1925 was the U.S. Open. It was scheduled for the first week in June in Worcester, Massachusetts at the Worcester Country Club. The sectional qualifying took place at three sites, one on the East Coast with 60 spots up for grabs, one in the Midwest where 35 would gain entry, and one on the West Coast where the top 5 would qualify. Sarazen, Hagen, and Bobby Jones were in the East Coast qualifier at the Lido Country Club on Long Island. The entries there were divided into two sections, with 30 from each section making the field. Hagen finished second in the first section. Bobby Jones, paired with Sarazen, won the second section. Sarazen struggled, but made the top 30 by two strokes.

At the Open a week later, Hagen, the reigning British Open and PGA champion, and Jones, who in his last three appearances in the event had two seconds and a first, were the favorites. In a practice round three days before the event, the two cofavorites made headlines. Playing together, Jones set a new record for the Worcester course with a round of 66, and Hagen recorded the first hole-in-one of his career.

Hagen's ace came at Worcester's sixth hole, which measured 180 yards and called for a blind tee shot over a knoll. When Hagen arrived on the tee, he noticed his ball had been damaged during the play of the previous hole. When he went to his bag to take out another ball, he discovered the cupboard was bare. After a few good-natured digs, Jones reached in his bag and tossed Hagen a ball. Hagen then pulled out one of his hickory-shafted irons from his bag. One of the shortcomings of the hickory shaft was that it tended to bend slightly when it was rattled around in the bag over the course of a round. Usually, this bend could be straightened out with a little pressure applied by the player, which Hagen attempted to do. Maybe this shaft had had it, or Hagen applied too much pressure; in any event, the shaft snapped in half. As one would expect, the Hagen/Jones pairing had a huge gallery following them, and it exploded in laughter. Hagen, known for being the one that generated laughter rather than being the butt of it, for a few seconds seemed quite the hapless fellow. He then reached in his bag and whipped out another club. He did not take the time to inspect the shaft on this one, but promptly addressed his ball and sent it over the hill. In a few seconds, the gallery at the green erupted into a wild cheering as the ball dropped into the cup.

While Hagen and Jones appeared to be peaking at just the right time, Sarazen's game was heading south. On the eve of the Open, he teamed up with McDonald Smith in a best ball match against Jock Hutchison and Hagen. For all practical purposes, the match was actually between Smith and the Hutchison/Hagen team with the latter winning handily, as Sarazen had no game that day.

Gene attributed his poor play to the fact that he was in flux both on and off the course. On the course, he was attempting to correct his disappointing play from the year before, and he believed a new grip and stance were the ticket. Gene's off-the-course issues included a civil lawsuit seeking damages of $50,000, which had been brought against him by the widow of the pedestrian he had fatally struck and killed in the fall of 1922. On top of this, a number of his investments had recently gone sour.

Once it began, the 1925 U.S. Open unfolded into the greatest Open to date and one of the greatest of all time. It is most remembered, however, for an occurrence during its opening round. One of the featured pairings of that round was that of the two players that had made the most noise during their practice rounds—Jones and Hagen. After they hit their opening drives and headed down the first fairway, most spectators in attendance were following along with them. By the time the twosome teed off on the 10th hole and headed down its fairway, they had very few followers, as both players appeared to have used up their best golf during their practice rounds.

Jones's decorum during his two major wins to date, the 1923 U.S. Open and the 1924 U.S. Amateur, had gone a long way in reconstructing his image from a foul-mouthed, club-throwing terror to one that was very positive. An occurrence on the back nine of the first round at Worcester would overnight propel Jones's image to that of the standard-bearer for propriety, sportsmanship, and fair play, not only in golf, but in all of sports.

On the par-four 11th hole, Jones's approach missed the green to the left and landed on an embankment in ankle-high rough. As he addressed his ball, which was visible to no one but himself, he thought it moved ever so slightly and he called a one-stroke penalty on himself. Jones, who had a three over par 39 on the front, finished his first round five over par, an opening score that did not portend him being a factor for the remainder of the event.

The pairing that had taken the gallery from Jones and Hagen was that of local hero Frances Ouimet, and Gene Sarazen. Ouimet was 12 years removed from his U.S. Open win, just a few miles away in Brookline, over Vardon and Ray. Now 33, Ouimet had remained an amateur. At this juncture, his game was as strong as ever. Ouimet finished his opening 18 with a score of two-under-par 70, which gave him the lead. His playing partner, Sarazen, had been given a pep talk by the friend who drove him to the course. The friend told Sarazen to forget his off-course problems and go back to the stance and grip that he used to win the 1922 Open at Skokie. He did and, if not for a double bogey on the 18th hole, he would have shared the first-round lead with Ouimet. As it was, he stood in a tie for third.

When the second round was completed that afternoon, Frances Ouimet slipped just a bit. Gene played another solid round. Leo Diegel, who had finished one stroke behind Ted Ray at the 1920 Open at Inverness, and Willie McFarlane, a journeyman pro from Scotland, had stellar second rounds and were the coleaders. Frances was one stroke behind in second and Gene was two strokes back in third. Bobby Jones had rallied in his second round, improving on his first round by six shots, and had moved into striking distance six shots away from the leaders.

McFarlane's showing was a bit of a surprise. He had not played in serious competition in over four years. His claim to fame was as an instructor to the immensely wealthy. Among his pupils were mining magnate Daniel Guggenheim and Otto H. Kahn, the wheeler-dealer Wall Street financier whose likeness became the symbol of the board game Monopoly.

Gene's playing partner for the final two rounds was an acquaintance from his caddying days, Johnny Farrell. The two had also played together on a baseball team formed by caddies. Another player on the caddie baseball team was Eddie Sullivan; he was now covering golf as a sportswriter for the *New York Evening Graphic*. He later would become known as Ed instead of Eddie and leave the sports page to cover entertainment. He would eventually create and host the long-running variety show on CBS Television, *The Ed Sullivan Show*.

In the third round, Sarazen fell back due to a rash of three-putting while Farrell surged. When the third round was over, MacFarlane had the lead with Farrell one stroke back. Ouimet, Jones, Diegel, and Hagen were all well within striking distance while Sarazen's chances appeared long.

It turned out Gene's chances were not as long as originally thought. He put on a charge, while the other leaders stalled or even fell back. But in the end, he came up two shots off the pace. Among the other contenders, Bobby Jones was first into the clubhouse at the time he signed his card. He was one stroke behind Willie MacFarlane, who was playing 16. MacFarlane bogeyed 16 and then parred in to finish in a tie with Jones. Ouimet, Farrell, and Hagen each came to the short par-four 18th hole needing birdie to tie, and each of them came up empty-handed.

MacFarlane and Jones met in the 18-hole play-off the following day for the title. They finished still tied. They played another 18 holes and MacFarlane came out the victor by one stroke when Jones failed to get up and down from a bunker at the final hole.

When it was over, much was made over how that one penalty shot proved so costly to Jones. He was lauded with compliments for his integrity and sportsmanship. Jones was uncomfortable with all the accolades and reportedly said, "You may as well praise a man for not robbing a bank."

When the U.S. Open finally concluded, the British Open, to be played at Prestwick in Scotland, was only three weeks away. But that was not a concern to Bobby Jones, Walter, or Gene. Bobby had not played in the event since he had torn up his card and stormed off the Old Course at St. Andrews in 1921. Gene was not going because of the state of his game. Walter, even though he was the defending champion, was not going either. He opted instead to make a three-week exhibition tour of northwest Canada.

When Gene took over as head professional at Fresh Meadow, he and Mary took up residence in a house in New Rochelle. A few days after returning from the Open in Worcester, Gene's problems away from the course increased. Driving in Yonkers, Mary struck a man as he was exiting his vehicle. She was not charged for hitting the man but was charged with driving without a license, and pleaded guilty in court a few weeks later and was given probation.

Things improved for Gene, at least on the golf course, several weeks after Mary's day in court. He won one of the oldest professional tournaments in the country, the New York City area's Metropolitan Open. The field featured almost all of the country's top professionals with the exception of Hagen, who was still on his Canadian tour. Gene fought off a challenge from Joe Turnsae in the fourth round to take the event by one stroke at the Grassy Sprain links in Bronxville, New York.

A month later Gene headed to Youngstown, Ohio, with high hopes to play in the second oldest professional golf tournament in the country: the Western Open. It was the country's third most prestigious professional tournament behind the U.S. Open and the PGA Championship. Four years younger than the U.S. Open, its venue changed from year to year from as far east as Ohio to as far west as Los Angeles. The 1925 edition was taking place in Youngstown at the Youngstown Country Club and included all the country's top professionals, including Hagen. The game that Gene had when he won the Metro did not make the trip, and he finished 13 strokes behind the winner, Macdonald Smith.

The PGA took place three weeks after the Western Open at Olympic Fields outside of Chicago. Gene arrived with low expectations, but his spirits were buoyed during the medal play qualifying when he qualified with ease for the 32-man match play field. His spirits were crushed the next day. His 1925 golf campaign ended on a very sour note when he was destroyed in his first match by Jack Burke by the count of eight holes down with seven to go.

Walter Hagen, the defending champion, won the event for his third PGA title.

7

WALTER'S GIFT

After Fresh Meadow closed down for the season, Mary and Gene returned to the Miami area for the winter, where Gene continued to tinker with his game, hoping to find the key that would again make him a major champion. When it came time to head north, Gene believed the key was still missing.

On the calendar for the major tournaments in 1926, the British Open and U.S. Open positions had flip-flopped. The British Open, which was being held at the Royal Lytham and St. Annes Golf Club on England's northwest coast, would lead off in late June. Thirteen days after its conclusion, the U.S. Open would take place at the Scioto Country Club in Columbus, Ohio.

Given the state of his game, Gene again decided not to make the Atlantic crossing for the British Open. Walter Hagen did make the voyage, and there was an addition to his traveling party. Recently, Walter had recorded another first in the annals of professional golf—he had become the first player to employ a caddie full time. The young lad's name was James McDonald.

A few days before the start of the Open Championship, Hagen took on one of Britain's top professionals, Abe Mitchell, in a 72-hole match play contest. With a payout of £2,000, it was the richest golf event that had ever taken place in the British Empire. The match took place over two days at two different courses in London. Mitchell was leading four-up after the first day.

On the second day, Hagen did not arrive on the first tee at the appointed time of 10:30. Mitchell paced around the teeing ground like a caged tiger, waiting on Hagen. At 10:55 Hagen arrived, but rendered no apology for his tardiness. After six holes, Mitchell's four-up lead had been erased. From that point on it was a nip-and-tuck battle until the 71st hole, when Mitchell hit a wayward approach shot and failed to get up and down to give Walter a two-up with one to go victory.

Six days later, Hagen pocketed just £40 for a third-place finish in the British Open. It would have been £20 less if the man he had tied for that position, American George Von Elm, had not been an amateur.

The winner of the Open Championship that year was another amateur, Bobby Jones. Jones had arrived in Great Britain a month before to play in the British Amateur and on America's Walker Cup team. He was originally scheduled to depart for the States three weeks ahead of the Open Championship, but after a poor showing in the British Amateur he decided to stay over and make his second appearance in a British Open.

Since the practice of pairing leaders in the third and fourth rounds was still decades away, it was by happenstance that Jones and Al Watrous, an American professional, were paired in the last two rounds. After round three, Watrous was the leader by two strokes over Jones. In the last round, it took Jones 16 holes to pull even with Watrous. Then thanks to three putts by Watrous at the 71st, Jones took the lead. Watrous three putted the 72nd hole to give Jones a two-stroke margin of victory in his first British Open win.

With Jones being an amateur, Watrous received the first-place purse of £70. Not only did he not receive winnings, but Jones also found it necessary to contribute to the Open Championship's revenue. After his morning third round on the second day of play, Jones had gone back to his hotel room to freshen up. Upon his return to the course, Jones discovered that he had forgotten his competitor's ticket. A by-the-book security guard, not recognizing Jones and not buying his explanation, refused him entry. Not wishing to push the point, Jones stepped over to a pay gate and purchased a spectator's ticket.

As Jones and Hagen were crossing the Atlantic on their return trip, Sarazen was working hard on his game in preparation for the U.S. Open. While Gene was on the course, he had lawyers working on one minor issue and one major issue. The minor issue was in magistrate's court; an attorney appeared for him and paid a $5 ticket for a moving violation. A few days before he had been given his ticket, Gene had appeared in the same magistrate court to represent Mary, who had again run afoul behind the wheel. This time she had been charged with operating a vehicle with faulty brakes. Gene produced evidence that the brakes on the vehicle had been repaired, and the magistrate suspended the charges.

The day after the minor issue in magistrate court was handled, Gene's attorneys reached a settlement in the civil case brought by the widow of the man who had died after being struck by Gene's vehicle back in the fall of 1922. The widow had been seeking $50,000, but she accepted $12,500 to resolve the matter before it went to trial.

At the U.S. Open at Scioto, Gene's combined score for the 36 holes played on the final day was a two-under-par 142, which was the best total of any player in the field. Unfortunately, Gene had been 11 over par after the first 36 holes. His strong finish did pull him into a five-way tie for third, four strokes out of first. The winner at Scioto was Bobby Jones, making him the first player to win the British Open and the U.S. Open in the same year. Jones's win came in dramatic fashion as he needed a birdie at the final hole to best Joe Turnesa by one stroke.

A few weeks later, Gene appeared to be well on his way to successfully defending his Metropolitan Open championship. The 1926 edition took place at the Salisbury Country Club in Garden City, New York. Gene had a three-stroke lead going into the final round, but bogeys at the 71st and 72nd holes dropped him into a tie with Macdonald Smith, forcing an 18-hole play-off the next day. The two were still tied at the play-off's conclusion. Another 18 holes were played and the two were still tied. The next morning, they teed up again for another 18 holes. Macdonald bogeyed the first hole, and then played the remaining 17 holes eight under and defeated Gene by three strokes.

The next event for Gene was the Canadian Open at the Royal Montreal Club in Montreal. After three rounds, he and his old buddy Johnny Farrell were tied for first, three strokes ahead of their nearest competitor. But they both fell apart in the final round, thanks in large part to getting caught in a violent thunderstorm. Gene ended up in second place, three strokes behind the man that had defeated him in the Metropolitan Open, Macdonald Smith, who had the good fortune to finish his final round just ahead of the storm.

A month later, the Highland Golf Club in Indianapolis, Indiana, was the site of the Western Open. With a fourth-place finish at the U.S. Open and two recent second-place finishes, Gene was listed as the favorite and held the 36-hole lead. In the third round, he shot an even par round and was passed like he was standing still by his archrival, Walter Hagen. Walter racked up four birdies on the back side on the way to setting a new course record with a score of 66, taking the lead. He played well in the final round while Gene struggled. When the day was over Walter had practically lapped the field. He was nine strokes ahead of Gene and Harry Cooper, who finished tied for second.

The PGA Championship followed the Western Open. It was taking place at the same venue that had hosted the Metropolitan Open two months before, the Salisbury Country Club on Long Island. Gene made an early exit, bowing out in the second round. Walter Hagen displayed the same form he had shown in the last two rounds of the Western Open and breezed through all of his five matches to win the event for the fourth time and the third time in succession.

At the last possible opportunity, Gene finally picked up a win in 1926. Down in Florida for the winter, he won the Miami Open on December 31st. Five days later; he got 1927 off on a high note by winning the Miami Beach Open.

Both of these victories had to be tempered a good bit, because both of the fields in these tournaments had only a smattering of top players. What momentum Gene had hoped to take with him into the coming season from these wins was snuffed out by Walter Hagen even before Gene had left Florida. The two staged a 72-hole match play contest with 36 holes being played in Miami, 18 holes in Sanford, Florida, and the final 18 at the Pasadena Country Club in Hollywood, Florida, a course in which Hagen had a substantial financial interest and served as its president.

When they started the final 18 holes at Walter's course, Gene was already eight down in the match. It officially ended on the front nine when Gene went 11 down after the eighth hole. So as to accommodate the large gallery that was present, they decided to play the 10 remaining holes. Walter continued to pound Gene, winning five of those holes and halving the rest.

The 1927 calendar of golf's foremost events would include a new addition—the Ryder Cup. It would have the lead-off position, taking place the first week in June at the Worcester Country Club in Worcester, Massachusetts. The U.S. Open would follow two weeks later at Oakmont. The British Open would take place in mid-July at the Old Course at St.

Andrews. The PGA Championship would not be held until much later in the year. It would start on October 31st. The host venue would be the Cedar Park Country Club in Dallas, Texas, marking the first time it would be played west of the Mississippi.

Gene and Walter departed Florida in late March and would play their way north in a series of exhibition matches. Walter was practically sporting an all-new wardrobe, not out of design but out of necessity. Several days before leaving Florida, Walter had gone to the St. Petersburg Police Department and sworn out a warrant for the young man he had hired as his full-time caddie the year before, James McDonald. In the warrant, Hagen contended that McDonald had gained entry to his apartment in St. Petersburg and had absconded with jewelry, cash, and a good chunk of Walter's wardrobe. It was also learned that McDonald had obtained money from several members of Hollywood Country Club under false pretenses. Police efforts to locate McDonald proved futile.

On the way north, Gene and Walter played in the Southern Open at Bobby Jones's home course, the East Lake Golf Club in Atlanta. Jones won the event by eight strokes. Both Walter and Gene played poorly. Walter finished 17 strokes behind Bobby. Gene was 22 strokes off the pace.

A week later at Pinehurst in the North-South Open, Walter had his game back. Gene did not. His shots seemingly were always going right, right into the pines. The reporter covering the event for the *New York Times* described his play as "sad." At the end of round two, Gene was 16 holes off the pace and withdrew. Walter, on the other hand, was tied with Emmett French for the lead. While he was on the course that day, a telegram from the PGA headquarters was sent out to him, offering him the captaincy of America's first Ryder Cup team. After concluding his round, Walter sent a telegram back to the PGA accepting the appointment.

On the final day of play at Pinehurst, Walter slipped a bit and ended up finishing in second place, two strokes behind the winner, Bobby Cruickshank.

After Pinehurst, Walter and Gene moved north to West Virginia's Greenbrier Resort where they had another head-to-head match scheduled. During an overnight stop on the way to Greenbrier, Walter announced that he planned to skip the British Open. Gene had already let it be known that he would, for the second straight year, skip the event as well.

In their 36-hole match at the Greenbrier, Gene defeated Walter two and one. But his win was somewhat blemished because Walter was playing with a bad foot. After the match, Walter had to seek out an orthopedic specialist who advised him to stay off the foot as much as possible for the next two weeks.

A few days after Greenbrier, the PGA of America announced the players that would be joining Walter on the Ryder Cup team. Gene was picked for the squad. The remainder of the team was Leo Diegel, Bill Melhorn, Mike Brady, Joe Turnesa, Al Watrous, Johnny Golden, Al Espinosa, and Johnny Farrell. The team reflected America's makeup as a melting pot, consisting of descendants of immigrants from England, Ireland, Poland, Germany, the Netherlands, Italy, and Spain. The PGA, however, excluded American citizens who were not born in the United States from being on the team. Among those left out because of this stipulation were McDonald Smith, who had won six tournaments the year before, and Tommy Armour, who was playing the best golf of his career.

At that first Ryder Cup at Worcester, the American squad trounced the British team nine and a half to two and a half. Al Watrous and Gene were victorious in the foursomes competition. Gene halved his match in the singles segment.

Two weeks later at the midway point of the U.S. Open at the Oakmont Country Club, Gene stood one stroke behind the leader, Harrison Johnston, an amateur from Minnesota. One stroke behind Gene was Tommy Armour. Two strokes behind Armour, Walter Hagen was lurking.

With 36 holes to be played the final day, those in the press tent believed that Sarazen was shaping up to be the man to beat, as it was suspected that Johnston would unravel under the pressure. There were also concerns about Armour standing up to the pressure. On the back nine in round two, he was already thought to be showing the strain, as he was taking six or seven waggles before pulling the trigger on his drives and approach shots.

The press was right about Johnston; he shot an 87 in round three. They were wrong about Sarazen being the man to beat as he bogeyed three of the first five holes on the way to a third-round score of 80. Armour, waggles and all, slipped just a touch. The top of the leaderboard now belonged to Harry Cooper, who was the class of the field in the third round. Armour was one stroke back in second. Walter Hagen was two strokes back in third. Sarazen, even with his third round 80, stood in fourth, four strokes back.

In the final 18 that afternoon, Walter faded. Gene put on a surge, while Harry Cooper and Tommy Armour struggled. Harry got to the clubhouse with a one-stroke lead. Gene briefly grabbed the lead on the back nine, then bogeyed 15 and 16 to drop one behind. He had makeable birdie putts at 17 and 18 but could not convert. Tommy's approach to the 18th green left him a 12-foot birdie putt to tie Harry. He drained it and then beat Harry the next day in an 18-hole play-off by three strokes to win his first major.

Tommy Armour's first-place money for winnings for the Open at Oakmont was $500. Gene took home $200 for his third-place finish. The golfer that left Oakmont with the most cash was Johnny Farrell, who took home $1,073. He received $73 for finishing in a four-way tie for seventh and $1,000 for the way he had dressed in the event. Johnny had joined Walter and Gene as the pro circuit's fashion leaders. An apparel company had put up $1,000 for the best-dressed competitor at Oakmont and Johnny had been judged the winner.

Bobby Jones's performance at Oakmont was not up to his recent standards in U.S. Open competition. He finished the first round six strokes off the pace and lingered in about that same position for the remaining three rounds. A month later, his play at the British Open was quite different. Defending the title he had won the year before at Royal Lytham in Lytham St. Annes, England, Jones returned to the Old Course at St. Andrews, the scene of his infamous meltdown in 1921. This time Jones stormed over St. Andrews, retaining his British Open crown and breaking the mark of lowest total score, which had stood for 18 years, by a half-dozen strokes with a 72-hole total of 285.

For Gene, the remainder of the 1927 campaign was an up-and-down affair. He won the Long Island Open by 11 strokes but the field for that event was thin talent-wise, with most of the top players absent, competing in the Canadian Open. At the Western Open at Olympia Fields in Chicago, he finished 16 strokes behind its winner—Walter Hagen. Against a top-flight field at Salisbury Country Club in Garden City, New York, Gene won the Metropolitan PGA by three strokes.

At the PGA Championship in Dallas, Gene posted victories in the first two rounds but fell in the quarterfinals to a fellow Italian, Joe Turnesa, four and three. Turnesa would make it to the finals, where he went up against Walter Hagen. Joe gave Walter all he could handle before losing the 36th and final hole to give Walter a one-up victory. The victory was Walter's fourth PGA title in a row and his fifth overall.

Approximately six months later, Gene was riding high. On a crisp early May afternoon, he was weighing his chances of getting a shot to carry the Suez Canal. Not the waterway in Egypt connecting the Mediterranean Sea to the Red Sea, but a namesake, a narrow stream that dissected the par-five 14th hole at Royal St. George's Golf Club at Sandwich, the site of the 1928 British Open. Normally a good drive and well-struck second shot would have easily carried the Suez but Gene's drive, although fine in the distance category, had landed in snarly rough. His caddie recommended that Gene just punch out with a short iron instead of risking having his ball find the bottom of the Suez. Gene stubbornly ignored his caddie's recommendation and asked for a fairway wood. It would be a decision that he would long regret.

In January, Gene had gotten 1928 off to a very good start. For the second year in a row, he had picked up back-to-back wins in the Miami Beach Open and the Miami Open. In March, he won the Bahamas Open, beating Johnny Farrell in a playoff. He was feeling good about his game, good enough so that he let it be known that he was going to be taking another crack at the British Open, which was taking place in early May, much sooner than usual. He pulled back from that decision a few weeks later on account of the shafts he had in his clubs. Gene, along with most of the country's top players, had switched from hickory shafts to shafts that were made with a combination of hickory and bamboo.

The R & A had not yet approved this type of shaft, so if Gene wanted to compete in the British Open, he would have to switch his shafts back to all hickory. He determined that making the switch and getting adjusted back to just hickory, then switching back once he returned and adjusting back to hickory and bamboo for the U.S. Open, would entail too much risk to his game and he decided that he would again skip the British Open.

Bobby Jones, the winner of the last two British Opens, had also decided to pass up the event. It looked like the American hopes in the Open Championship would fall on the shoulders of Walter Hagen, Wild Bill Melhorn, and Tommy Armour, but at the last minute they were reinforced by Gene after he experienced an eleventh-hour change of heart. During the couple of weeks since he had decided not to go, his game had only gotten better. Despite the shaft issue, he was just playing too well not to go.

Walter and Gene sailed over on the *Aquitania.* One evening on their six-day voyage, Gene emerged from one of the ship's lounges with his chances of winning the British Open greatly enhanced. He and Walter had spent some time after dinner sharing drinks and discussing the Open Championship. Near the end of their discussion, Walter did something that for the all-time king of gamesmanship was quite uncharacteristic—he gave Gene a gift, one that he believed was the key for any American golfer to have shot at winning the British Open: a top-notch caddie.

Hagen had already made arrangements for Skip Daniels, the veteran British caddie that had been on his bag when he won his first British Open in 1922, to caddie for him at Royal St. George's. Daniels was in his early 60s and had caddied at Sandwich's two championship courses, Prince's and Royal St. George's, for as long as anyone could remember. He knew the courses and how they should be played better than anyone.

That night in the lounge, Walter decided to give Gene Daniels's services for the British Open. To say the least, it was a very generous gesture and certainly not one that matched up with Walter's profile. He appeared to be mellowing out. During the late fall and winter, he had played very little golf at all. He had spent a generous amount of his time during that period in a failed attempt to buy the Rochester, New York, baseball team of the International League. He had also recently parted ways with his long-time business manager.

When they arrived in England, Walter and Gene went to London. Gene spent a few days there and then departed for Sandwich to connect with Skip Daniels and begin practicing for the Open Championship, which was two weeks away. Walter stayed behind. He was scheduled to play in a much-ballyhooed match against one of England's top professionals, Archie Compston.

At Royal St. George's, Gene advised the caddie master of Hagen's gift and had his first meeting with Daniels, who was more than a little disappointed that he would not be teaming with Hagen. But Skip seemed to get over his disappointment in short order, as he and Gene developed a good chemistry from the start. Skip's disappointment may have also been tempered by what happened to Walter in his match against Archie Compston. In a match play contest scheduled for 72 holes, Walter rewrote the meaning of going down in flames, being closed out at the 55th hole when he fell 18 holes behind with 17 holes to play.

Compston's utter rout of Hagen spurred the hopes of the home crowd for a golfer on the home team taking the British Open. In six of the last seven Open Championships an American had claimed the title.

Gene and Walter, whose game had come around after some earnest practice, both made it through the 36-hole qualifier with ease. Rounds one and two would take place on separate days and rounds three and four would take place on the final day. Fellow American Wild Bill Melhorn had the lead after day one. Gene had the second spot, one stroke back, and Walter was just two behind Gene.

In the second round, Melhorn fell back and Josè Jurado from Argentina, an early starter, put on a burst from the pack and grabbed the lead. Gene was on his back nine and on a pace to surpass José when he reached the par-five 14th, the longest hole on the course and the home of the infamous Suez Canal. Gene pulled his tee ball a shade and it left him with a bad lie in the snarly rough. He surveyed his second shot, glancing at the Suez Canal out in the distance and then down at his ball. He formed the opinion that despite the ball's lie, he could get a fairway wood up with enough oomph to carry the Suez. When he looked over at his highly knowledgeable and experienced caddie, Skip was tapping his finger on a mid-iron, indicating that punching out into the fairway was what Gene needed to do. Gene balked. He told Skip if he cleared the Suez he would almost be guaranteed the lead. Skip's retort was that he didn't need the lead that day. He needed it at the end of play on the following day.

Gene ignored Skip's sage counsel and asked for the wood. Skip complied. A minute later, Gene was surveying his next shot, again trying to decide whether he could carry the Suez Canal. His last shot had been dreadful. The club had been grabbed by the thick rough and his ball had traveled a mere 20 feet, still in the rough and still resting in a bad way. Stubbornly, he went for clearing the Suez again. The shot came out with questionable propulsion. With Bobby Jones not in the field, the lion's share of the gallery had chosen Gene as the player to follow. This sizeable throng let out a collective groan as Gene's ball disappeared as it crossed the front edge of the Suez.

The result was bad for sure but not as bad as it could have been, as Gene's ball had avoided the Suez's water and plugged into its bank on the far side. Gene was able to slash his ball out of the bank and onto the fairway. He then put his fifth shot on the green and two-putted for a double-bogey. Gene finished with all pars. At day's end, despite his self-inflicted wound at the 14th hole, he remained firmly in the hunt, resting just two strokes off the pace of the leader, José Jurado, in a tie for second place with Walter Hagen.

The last two rounds on the final day shaped up to be a shootout between Walter, José, and Gene. Hagen had the hot hand in the third round that morning. He slipped into the lead by one stroke over Gene and José. Gene was striking the ball well that morning and he was confident that he would overtake Walter—so confident that he went to his room during the break between rounds and wrote out an acceptance speech. He needed it to be extra sharp as the Prince of Wales, the man who would later become King Edward VIII and then give up his throne to marry Wallis Simpson, an American divorcee, would be in attendance.

Gene had an avid golfer from the States who was staying at the same hotel read over his acceptance speech to make sure it fit the occasion. This individual worked in Hollywood and would soon be on his way to becoming motion-picture royalty, winning four Oscars for best director. The most acclaimed of those four were *The Grapes of Wrath* and *How Green Was My Valley*. He would also be the director of the John Wayne blockbuster, *Stagecoach*. His name was John Ford.

Gene had been one of the last groups to go out in the morning round. When he was on the way to the ninth tee, a member of the gallery got what Gene felt was a little too chatty with Skip. When they reached the tee, Gene asked Skip, "Who was that guy?" Skip told him it was a frequent visitor to Sandwich for whom he had often caddied. He was quite a pleasant fellow. This gentleman was also considered to be the Crown's most high-profile golfer, and he was also the heir to the crown. He was the Prince of Wales. Skip then took Gene over to the prince for a quick introduction.

The then 34-year-old prince had been slow to take to golf. Up until his late 20s, his game was weak and his interest in it even weaker. That changed in the summer of 1923, when he took a vacation cottage in Sandwich, a stone's throw away from the Royal St. George's and the Prince's courses. Early during his stay, the prince ventured onto one of the two courses and began striking the ball as he had never done before. He had distance. He had accuracy. And most importantly, he had consistency. He was amazed at his sudden turnaround from a Royal hacker into someone who actually looked like he belonged on the links. He couldn't wait to share the news about his golfing transformation at Sandwich, firing off a note to one of his best friends back in London triumphantly declaring he had found his "permanent swing." Thus, virtually overnight, he had experienced a conversion from casual golfer to full-fledged golf fanatic of the highest order.

Reports of the prince's golf activity were seemingly in the press every day. To avoid being criticized by the clergy and the press for playing golf on Sunday, he would slip into his small four-seater plane on Sunday morning and make the short hop across the English Channel to France to get in a round.

At no time was the prince's golf obsession more obvious than during his travels across the globe representing the Crown. While on a tour of Egypt, he hit a drive at the Great Pyramid. In the eastern Africa country of Uganda, despite the fact he was recovering from a bout with malaria, he drove 180 miles to reach one of that country's few courses. In Bermuda, the guests at an elaborate arrival luncheon in his honor were told to go ahead and dine without him. He was going to skip lunch so he would have time to get in 18 holes before dark at the island's famous Mid-Ocean course.

Much of the time when the prince traveled, it was with a small British armada, which proved to be beneficial for a number of the members of the Anglo-American Coffee Merchants Country Club in Santos, Brazil. While playing their course, the prince made a hole-in-one. He joyously paid the usual penalty: drinks all around the house. Then, to extend the celebration, he sent word to the captain of his flagship on the trip, the aircraft carrier *Eagle*, to send over a case of Scotch whisky from the ship's stores.

In the final round at the Open Championship, José Jurado was out first in the final round. Walter went out 30 minutes later. Gene started an hour behind Walter. José self-destructed with an 80. Walter was in sand seven times during his round but still shot an even par 72. When he finished his round, he and the prince, with whom he had become fast friends during one of his previous trips, headed back out on the course to follow Gene's play over his last six holes. Gene was one stroke behind Walter at that point and needed a birdie down the stretch to tie. But he played the last six holes one over to finish alone in second place, two strokes behind Walter.

As Gene stood and watched the Prince of Wales hand the Claret Jug to Walter, he had to be thinking about what might have been had he not thrown away two strokes by not taking Skip's advice on the 14th hole in the second round.

8

JUST SOUTH OF THE BORDER

Three hundred and sixty-four days later, Gene stood near the 18th green at Muirfield in Scotland and watched Walter Hagen accept the Claret Jug for the fourth and final time. Gene likely took solace in the fact that, unlike the 1928 Open Championship, his performance at Muirfield had not produced another one of those oh-so-close occasions. He finished in a tie for the eighth spot, 12 shots behind Walter.

Gene's play at Muirfield fit the pattern for his play on golf's biggest stages over the last 12 months—he could not put together a solid performance. He would start off strong, then dig himself into a hole and try and play catch-up. Here at Muirfield, he was in striking distance of Hagen after 36 holes, but an 81 in the third round butchered his chances.

Six weeks after his misfortune in the 1928 Open Championship at Royal St. George's, he stumbled out of the gate in the U.S. Open at Olympia Fields. But over the last 36 holes, he was one of the sharpest players in the field and finished in a tie for sixth. Bobby Jones and Gene's good friend, the dapper Johnny Farrell, finished in a tie after 72 holes. In a 36-hole play-off the following day, Farrell claimed the title by one stroke, when he sank an eight-foot birdie putt at the final hole.

Later that summer at the PGA Championship in Baltimore, Gene won his first three matches and then was destroyed by the eventual winner, Leo Diegel, in the semifinal by the shaming count of nine down with eight to go.

Off the course, Gene had a heart-stopping moment behind the wheel in late October. He was driving through Harlem when a six-year-old boy ran in front of his car and was knocked to the pavement. Gene scooped up the lad and drove him to the Harlem Hospital. He was checked over and his injuries were found to be minor. Gene wasn't charged for hitting the boy, but he did receive a ticket for not having his driver's license in his possession.

In late November the captain of the Ryder Cup team for the match in Britain in the coming May was announced at the PGA annual meeting in Cleveland. You would have thought that, given his resume, Gene would have been a prime candidate for the post, but the nod went to Leo Diegel, the recent winner of the PGA Championship. Diegel declined the appointment, stating that he believed Walter Hagen, who had captained the first Ryder Cup team in 1927, was a much better man for the job. The delegates went along with Diegel's suggestion and named Walter the captain.

Again, Gene got his new year off to a good start. In the first week in January he won, for the third year in a row, the Miami Open, almost lapping the field with an eight-stroke margin over the second-place finisher. The following week he won, also for the third year in a row, the Miami Beach Open. This win came in dramatic fashion when he dropped a 35-foot birdie putt on the last hole to win by one stroke.

In Flushing, New York, on a warm summer's night in late June, seven weeks after departing Muirfield, New York, Gene slipped into bed for the evening tied for the lead in the U.S. Open after 36 holes. Thanks to the Open being played at the Winged Foot Golf Club in nearby Mamaroneck, New York, he had the added pleasure of sleeping in his own bed.

Perhaps no one was more surprised than Gene about his showing in the first two rounds. He was struggling coming into the Open. The club that was letting him down the most was his driver. On the eve of the tournament, he decided he would take that club out of his bag and use a fairway wood or long iron off the tee.

Gene's strategy was to play smart and take no unnecessary chances, and this strategy paid off. He shot a one-under-par 71. Gene was one of only three players to break par. The other two were the leader, Bobby Jones, who shot an opening round of 69, and Al Espinosa, who fired a 70 to grab second place. In his round Gene had an eagle on the fifth hole and on the back side he was the up and down king, using just 11 putts.

In the second round Gene and Al Espinosa had early tee times. Gene shot another rock-solid 71. Espinosa fell back and posted a 72. Their scores of 142 put them on top of the leaderboard. First-round leader Bobby Jones had a late tee time. He got caught in a heavy late-afternoon rain and his scoring suffered. He posted a 75 to drop back to third, two strokes behind the two leaders.

The Winged Foot Golf Club is one of the game's most highly revered locales. In its hosting of major events, it has provided some treasured moments for a number of the game's top professionals and amateurs. Winged Foot is also believed to have given the duffers who play the game something as well—the mulligan. It is a do-over shot used frequently by casual and weekend golfers that is taken without penalty. As the story goes, one morning a member of Winged Foot named Mulligan misfired his opening drive on the first hole and re-teed another ball. He called his second drive a "correction shot." His playing companions that day decided it needed a better name. They dubbed it a "mulligan."

For the opening drive of the 36-hole final day in the 1929 Open, Gene could have certainly used a mulligan. Gene made an ill-fated decision before he even teed off: he put his driver back in his bag. Gene used it from the first tee and his drive missed the fairway by a wide margin, landing in ankle-high clover which led to an opening bogey. For the rest of the third round, he struggled and came in with a 76. Al Espinosa struggled as well. He came home with a 77. Bobby played well, shooting a 71 and taking the lead. Gene had second all alone, three shots back. Al was in third, four back.

In the final round, Al was out first, followed 15 minutes later by Gene. Bobby started an hour later. Al got to the clubhouse in less-than-sterling fashion with a 75. Gene appeared to be coming on early in his final round until his driver let him down again. A roping hook at the sixth hole led to a double bogey. He struggled home from that point and finished with a 78.

As the afternoon progressed, Espinosa's closing round began to actually look better and better, as Jones was struggling. Jones reached the 18th tee needing a birdie to win and a par to tie. His birdie chances flew away with his approach into a greenside bunker. His explosion left him 12 feet from the hole and par was anything but assured. Jones gathered himself and rolled his ball into the hole to force a play-off.

With his driver out of his bag, Gene was two under for the first 36 holes of the Open. With it in his bag for the final 36 holes, he was 10 over. Even with his difficulties in the last two rounds, Gene finished just two strokes short of joining Espinosa and Jones in the playoff.

The next day in the 36-hole tiebreaker, Jones claimed the most lopsided win in the annals of golf play-offs. After the first 18, he held a 12-shot advantage. In the afternoon session, Jones backed off just slightly, taking that 18 by 11 strokes. The final count for the day was Jones 141 and Espinosa 164.

Over the next two months, Gene picked up two top 10 finishes in tournaments, but in both cases he was well off the pace.

In early September, the U.S. Amateur was taking place at Pebble Beach and Bobby Jones was, of course, the heavy favorite. But Jones was knocked out in the first round of the match play event, in one of the upsets of the ages in golf, by Johnny Goodman, a lightly regarded (at the time) 20-year-old amateur from Nebraska.

Three days later and 3000 miles to the east, Gene went down to an unheralded lightweight in the New York City area's Metropolitan Open, which was now a match play event.

Gene was making a strong run in the event. He advanced into the semifinals where he went up against 20-year-old Walter Kozak, who was the Cinderella story of tournament. Kozak had received his PGA member card only three days before the start of the tournament. His performance was being driven by a club he had borrowed from a friend, a square-headed aluminum putter.

Against Gene, with a bandana tied over his head, Kozak's putting remained hot. In their match that he closed out at the 16th green with a three-and-two advantage, Kozak had nine one-putt greens. He won the tournament the next day, beating Joe Turnsae in the finals.

If the defeat at the hands of Kozak wasn't bad enough, Gene barely missed another embarrassing moment a week later. The PGA Championship was to take place in early December in Los Angeles. Qualifying for the Northeast section of the PGA took place a week after the Metropolitan Open at the Knollwood Golf Club in White Plains, New York. Eighty-two pros were vying for 11 spots over 36 holes. Gene almost didn't make it. He shot 80 in the first 18. He bore down in the second 18 and shot a 71. This left him in a three-way tie for the 11th spot, which he claimed on the third hole of a play-off.

The 1929–1930 winter circuit was the largest in history in number of events, the lengthiest in miles and days, and also the richest. It kicked off in late October in Oklahoma City, two days before the stock market crashed and the Great Depression began. From Oklahoma, the tour moved to Portland and then to Honolulu for the Hawaiian Open Championship. From Honolulu, it was back to Los Angeles and the PGA Championship. After several other California events, it would wrap up its West Coast swing 20 miles from San Diego and 3 miles into Mexico with the most anticipated event on its schedule, the Agua Caliente Open at the Agua Caliente Resort.

The resort, which was being billed as the "Monte Carlo of the Americas," was being spearheaded by Baron Long, a former small-time bad boy who had risen to be a major player in nightclubs, gambling, hotels, and horse racing. Agua Caliente had opened the year before, featuring a casino and a horse racing track. Golf was added in the spring of 1929 and Leo Diegel, the 1928 PGA champion, was brought in as its professional. Shortly before the course opened, Long announced that in January 1930 it would be the site of the richest professional golf tournament ever held.

In a time when a total purse on the tour was between $5,000 and $7,500 and the winner's take ranged from $750 to $1,200, the Agua Caliente was going to have a total purse of $25,000, with $10,000 going to the winner. These numbers had the pro golf community drooling.

Gene was late hooking up with the tour, arriving on the West Coast in mid-November, just in time to sail for the Hawaiian Open. In Hawaii, he finished fourth. The next stop was the PGA Championship in Los Angeles. Gene made it to the third round where he ran up against the new Agua Caliente pro, Leo Diegel, who had drubbed him nine and eight in the semifinals in the 1928 PGA. Diegel again came out on top, but it was a much tighter contest this time, with the final count being three-up with two to go. Diegel won his next two matches to claim his second straight PGA title.

After the PGA, Gene decided to skip the remaining events on the West Coast swing, including the rich Agua Caliente, and return to his winter home base, Miami, then pick up the tour again when it reached Florida in mid-February.

The first week in January, while the winter circuit was playing the Long Beach Open, Gene and the other professionals that were wintering in Florida took part in the Miami Open. Gene made three eagles on the last day to come from five strokes back to win the event for the fourth consecutive year. His first-place check was $750.

After that closing-day performance in Miami, Gene's instincts told him he needed to go back to the West Coast and go after the big money at Agua Caliente. It would prove to be a very wise decision.

A field of 114 teed off on a Monday at Agua Caliente. The course proved to be quite the challenge. It was long and wound its way through windswept canyons. On its par-71 layout, 48 of those players failed to break 80. No one broke par. The leader by one stroke was Ed Dudley at level par 71. Gene was four strokes back with a 75.

A group of nine golfers were in with 74s. One player in this group, Harry Cooper, was allowed to play nine holes of his second round that same day. This was the result of an agreement Cooper had reached with the organizers of the tournament. He was not going to be present for the second round, because after those nine holes Cooper was going to make the 140-mile trip to Los Angeles. The next day he was going to marry Emma Buchanan, whom he had met two years earlier on the West Coast swing. He would return to Agua Caliente for the third day of the event and play 27 holes to catch up with the rest of the field.

On the second day, again, no player broke par. Dudley faded. Olin Dutra was the new leader, and Sarazen found himself in a six-way tie for third, two behind Dutra.

Extremely windy conditions prevailed in round three, so much so that tournament officials changed the par-five eighth hole to a par six. Only four players in the field parred the 435-yard, par-four first hole and only two players made par at the 445-yard, par-four 18th. Al Espinosa shot the best round of the day, a 76, which put him in a tie for the lead with Horton Smith. Dutra dropped back into a three-way tie for second, one stroke back. Gene, one of the two players that parred the 18th, was four shots off the pace.

Harry Cooper had shot 36 on the front nine of his second round before departing for his wedding. He went off early that morning on his second-round back nine and shot a 43. In his third round, he posted a 77, which left him five strokes behind the two leaders.

In the final round, Gene took command of the tournament on the front nine. After two up and downs to save pars in the first three holes, he birdied three of the remaining six holes for a 32 going out. Gene let a half-dozen other players back into the chase when he double-bogeyed the 10th hole and bogeyed the 11th. Things remained tight until Gene put on a closing burst similar to his charge at Skokie in his 1922 U.S. Open win.

He birdied 15, 16, and 17 to win by two strokes. His closing-round score of 68 was a course record, and one of only two rounds in the tournament under par. The other, a one under 70, was turned in by amateur George Von Elm, who had beaten Bobby Jones in the finals of the 1926 U.S. Amateur.

Gene did not leave Agua Caliente with all of his $10,000 in winnings. Before the tournament, he had entered into an agreement with Johnny Farrell and Leo Diegel; if one of them won, the winner would give the other two $1,000.

Newlywed Harry Cooper finished in a tie for 13th place and took home $200. His union to Emma would last until his death 70 years later in 2000. Emma passed away in 2002.

A few weeks after the Agua Caliente, Gene and the rest of the touring golf professionals got a big break from the Bureau of Internal Revenue, as it was called at that time. It issued a ruling that golf pros were engaged in a profession and, beginning with their 1930 tax returns, they would be allowed to deduct travel and lodging expenses and equipment costs. The cost of apparel was not included.

In early March, when the tour passed through Florida, Gene picked up another victory, the Florida West Coast Open in Belleair, Florida. He won in the same fashion as he had won earlier in the year at Miami and at Agua Caliente, putting on a charge on the last day to grab the win.

Gene's last stop on the way north was Augusta, Georgia, for the Southeastern Open. The tournament's 72 holes were played on two courses and jammed into two days. On the first day, Augusta Country Club was the site. Gene shot an even par 72 in his first round, but ballooned to an 82 in round two. At the third and fourth rounds, played the next day at the Forest Hills-Ricker course, he continued to struggle with scores of 79 and 78. He finished 27 strokes behind the winner. Gene's performance at Augusta did not portend a big slide downhill. Over the rest of 1930, he would notch five more victories to finish with a total of eight for the year. This total would have been news in any other year— but this was far from any other year.

The winner whom Gene had finished 27 strokes behind in Augusta was Bobby Jones. His victory there would be one of five he would win that year; the other four were the British Amateur, the British Open, the U.S. Open, and the U.S. Amateur, his Grand Slam.

Gene had made the decision early in the year not to compete in the British Open at the Royal Liverpool Golf Club in Hoylake. He waivered a bit after his win at the Florida West Coast Open, but then decided to stick to his original decision. The American professionals made a strong showing at Hoylake with Leo Diegel, Macdonald Smith, and Horton Smith finishing second, third, and fourth respectively behind Jones, the amateur.

Four weeks later at the Interlachen Country Club near Minneapolis, Bobby captured the U.S. Open. He took command in the third round. There were a few anxious moments for him coming home on the final back nine but he came away with a two-stroke victory. Gene's play at Interlachen was far from top drawer. A double bogey on the 18th hole in the first round seemed to rock his game. At tournament's end, Gene was 19 strokes behind Bobby in a tie for 28th.

After his poor showing at Interlachen, Gene rebounded. He won a 36-hole one-day tournament in Philadelphia by one stroke, thanks to a five-birdies-in-a-row burst on the front nine of his second 18. A month later, Gene picked up his lone win in the Western Open. The host site was the Indian Wood Golf Club in Detroit. Gene's victory came in convincing fashion, as he was seven strokes ahead of the second-place finisher. His 72-hole score of 10-under-par 278 established a new record for the event.

A few weeks later Gene won again, taking the J. J. Lannin Memorial Open on Long Island. This win was particularly sweet, as the player he overtook on the back nine of the final round to take a one-stroke victory was Walter Kozak, the young pro who had knocked him out of the PGA Championship the year before.

The 1930 PGA Championship kicked off three days after the Lannin Memorial. Given his run of three recent victories and the fact that the PGA was being played at Fresh Meadow, where he had been head professional for the last six years, Gene had to feel good about his chances. These two big pluses didn't seem to matter in his first match. He struggled against an upstart young pro from Philadelphia by the name of Charles Schneider. The match went the full 36 holes before Gene claimed the win, one-up. In the next three rounds, he had a relatively easy time of it and cruised into the final match.

Gene faced off against Tommy Armour in the final match. The two had become close friends over the years. As they stood on the first tee, their well-earned reputations as golf fashion plates were on full display. It had been Amour's wife, Consuelo, who had put Gene on the road to good fashion during that conversation back in 1922, but Consuelo wasn't at Fresh Meadow that day. She and Tommy had gone through a messy divorce. She had made headlines in the spring when she filed court papers seeking $670,000 from Tommy. Consuelo eventually ended up settling for a lesser amount.

Tommy and Gene's final match was a nip-and-tuck affair. Tommy's game from the tee and on approach shots was much stronger than Gene's. But on the greens, Gene was solid while Tommy struggled. He had numerous opportunities from the four- to seven-foot range to win holes but seemingly could not buy a putt. When they reached the 36th and final hole, the match was all square. After their tee shots, Tommy had the advantage. He was in the fairway while Gene had found a fairway bunker. Tommy's outlook seemed even better after Gene sent his shot from the fairway bunker into a bunker in front of the green. But that outlook changed to an even affair when Tommy put his approach in the same front green bunker.

After their bunker shots, Gene had a slight advantage. He was 10 feet from the cup; Tommy was 12. Tommy stroked the putt with the confidence of a man who had made everything he had stood over on the previous 35 holes. It went right in the heart of the cup. Gene missed.

Now seven years removed from his last major victory, Gene had to be wondering if he would ever claim another one. A little over two weeks later, Bobby Jones, who had won three U.S. Opens and three British Opens since Gene's last big win at the PGA in 1923, closed out his Grand Slam with a victory at the U.S. Amateur at Oakmont. Two months later, Jones announced his retirement from competitive golf.

Gene made a change in his schedule for the coming winter circuit. He would go forgo his usual early January schedule of tournaments in the Miami area and would play the full West Coast swing.

When the final tally for the 1930–1931 winter circuit was posted, Gene was the leading money winner with $8,332, edging out George Von Elm by $375. It should not have been this close. Von Elm finished second in the second edition of the big payout Agua Caliente Open, losing to Johnny Golden in an 18-hole play-off. The winner's purse, as it had been the year before for Gene, was $10,000. Second place paid $3,500; however, Von Elm left Agua Caliente with a total of $6,750 in winnings because he and Golden agreed to split first and second place money before their play-off began.

Gene took home $500 from Agua Caliente for finishing in a 10th-place tie with old rival Walter Hagen and the future victim of his shot heard around the world, Craig Wood.

The lion's share of Gene's winnings for the season came from golf's second-richest payday, the Miami Beach–La Groce Open. The event was underwritten by the City of Miami Beach. It had a $15,000 purse with $5,000 going to the winner. Gene captured the winner's check on the back nine when he overtook the man who had edged him out of the 1930 PGA title, Tommy Armour, to win by two strokes.

At the close of 1930, Gene had ended his employment with Fresh Meadow Country Club. When the tour wrapped up in late March 1931, Gene took over the head professional duties at the Lakeville Country Club on Long Island.

Over the winter, Gene had decided to make another run at the British Open. The 1931 edition was taking place in early June at the Carnoustie Golf Links in Scotland. With Bobby Jones in retirement and not defending his 1930 title, Gene, Johnny Farrell, and Macdonald Smith were given the best chance from the American contingent. Henry Cotton, Archie Compston, and Percy Allis were the top picks from Great Britain's ranks.

Gene was two strokes off the pace after round one and stayed at or around that point for the entire tournament. He would finish in a tie for third with England's Percy Allis, two strokes behind the winner, who was an American that didn't make the favorites list—Tommy Armour.

Ten days after Carnoustie, Gene was in Ohio. The Buckeye State was going to be the center of the golf world for the next three weeks. First, Gene was going to defend his Western Open title at the Miami Valley Golf Club in Dayton. A week later in Columbus, the third Ryder Cup was to take place. Walter Hagen would again captain the squad, and Gene had been one of the top selections for the team. The following week, Gene would return to the locale and the event where he began his major championship golf career, Inverness in Toledo and the U.S. Open.

From the first round to the finish, the Western Open was a two-man race between Ed Dudley and Walter Hagen. Dudley pulled away in the final round to win. Hagen was four strokes back in second. Gene was seven strokes back in the same position he had been in the British Open, a tie for third.

The American team romped over the British at the Ryder Cup by a count of nine to three. On day one in the foursome matches, Gene and

Johnny Farrell destroyed their opposition eight-up with seven to go. In the singles matches the next day, Gene rolled over his opponent seven-up with six to go.

With third-place finishes in the British Open and Western Open and his stellar performance in the Ryder Cup, Gene arrived in Toledo feeling good about his chances in the Open. In the final round, he became one of two players to break par in the tournament when he shot a one-under-par 70. It was too little too late. He had shot a 78 in round two and faced a difficult climb to catch the leaders. His final round lifted him into a four-way tie for fourth place, four strokes behind George Von Elm and Billy Burke, who were tied for first at the end of regulation. Von Elm and Burke's play-off was the longest in U.S. Open history. It lasted for 72 holes over two days, with Burke prevailing by one stroke.

At the PGA Championship at the Wannamoisett Country Club in Rumford, Rhode Island, in mid-September, over 100 PGA pros took part in the 36-hole medal play to determine who would advance to the final 32 spots of match play. Gene bested them all. He then breezed through his first three matches to reach the semifinals.

Gene's opponent in the semifinals was 20-year-old Tom Creavy from Albany, New York. At the start of the event, he had been considered the darkest of dark horses, but after impressive wins in his first three matches, Creavy now had the look of a thoroughbred. In their 36-hole match, he spotted Gene a two-up lead early in the match and then blew by him on the way to a five-up with three to go win.

Creavy went on to defeat Denny Shute in the finals. It would be his only major win, as his career would be cut short by back problems.

Gene did pick up a win before the season ended. It came at the Lannin Memorial on Long Island, an event he had also won the year before. This win was the 30th of his career, but 26 of these wins had come after his last major win. Having won three of the first seven majors he played, Gene had gone 0 for 20 since 1923. He had certainly been in striking distance plenty of times, as over that stretch of majors he had two seconds, four thirds, one fifth, and a sixth. Each passing year, the pressure to win another was increasing. There was a sentiment building that Gene was now snakebit in the majors, and that there might not be an antidote to be had.

9

REUNITED

The Los Angeles Open kicked off the winter tour's 1932 calendar. Gene finished in a four-way tie for third, five strokes behind the winner. The third rendition of the Agua Caliente Open was the next stop. Fred Morrison, an unheralded pro from Culver City, California, shocked everyone when he walked away with the scaled-back $5,000 first prize. Gene finished two strokes behind him in second and took home a check for $2,500.

As the tour made its way east, Gene finished fifth in Phoenix and second in the Texas Open at San Antonio. He pulled out a one-stroke victory at the tour's next stop, the New Orleans Open. It was in New Orleans that Gene won the Southern Open in 1922, kicking off a year that would see him win his first two majors. Despite his recent strong play, it would have been difficult for anyone to fathom that history was going to repeat itself, as Gene would claim his second U.S. Open and would substitute his win in the 1922 PGA Championship for an even more prestigious title—the British Open.

The financial commitment and time required to make the trip had Gene lukewarm about taking a shot at the 1932 British Open. Only a smattering of American pros had indicated they were going. Walter Hagen was taking a pass for the third year in a row. Gene's wife Mary, on the other hand, was a different story. Since their honeymoon trip to the 1923 British Open, Mary had seen how much the event meant to her husband. Because of Gene's strong play on the winter tour, she was all in for another go for the British Open. To save on cost, she volunteered to stay home.

Mary's push won the day. In mid-May, Gene sailed for the Open Championship, which was to be played in three weeks at the Prince's Golf Club in Sandwich. Gene had more faith in his game than at any time since his two major wins in 1922. One reason for his high level of confidence could be attributed to a new addition to his bag. He called it a sand iron. We call it today a sand wedge.

In the 1987 Masters, Larry Mize arguably pulled off the second most famous shot in golf history. From 140 feet, he used a sand wedge to chip in for birdie at Augusta's par-four 11th hole to defeat Greg Norman in a play-off. Although Mize was not in a bunker, the sand wedge's design has made the club one of the golfer's best tools for pitches and short shots. In an ironic twist, the man who had perfected the sand wedge was the man who had hit the most famous shot in golf history: Gene Sarazen.

Bunker play had always been a weak spot in Gene's game. He was not alone. Most of his fellow competitors on tour would have considered it their weak spot as well. And for the average golfer at this time, escaping from a sand trap was a very tall order. The chief reason for this was that no club in the bag was up to the task. Up until the late 1920s, most players used the niblick, equivalent to today's 9-iron, when they found themselves in a greenside bunker. Bobby Jones sometimes would use a mashie, a 5-iron today, with the blade wide open. In 1928, golfers received some welcome relief when a Texan by the name of Edwin Kerr MacClain invented and patented a club specifically designed for the sand.

A member of the Houston Country Club, MacClain had a penchant for landing in sand traps. Frustrated by the fact that there was nothing more useful than a niblick for extricating his ball from the sand, MacClain took matters into his own hands and designed a sand wedge. The club was far from a joy to the eye. It had a strange concave face and it resembled a large ice cream scoop on a stick. But it certainly got the job done, and golfers of all stripes snapped it up. In 1929, Horton Smith, who would win the first Masters in 1934, had it in his bag that season and posted eight wins.

In early 1930, Smith won the Savannah Open, beating Bobby Jones by one stroke. After the tournament, Smith gave Jones a MacClain sand wedge. It would prove to be a very valuable addition to Jones's bag. Four months later in the final round of the British Open at Hoylake, the second leg of his Grand Slam, Jones had a two-stroke lead when he teed off at the 16th hole but hit a wayward approach shot that left his ball in a nasty lie in a greenside bunker near its lip. Jones took the MacClain sand wedge out of his bag. The lie forced him to stand with one foot in the sand and the other on a grassy slope. He then proceeded to hit what many considered the shot of the tournament. His blast from the sand stopped four inches from the cup, and for all practical purposes a Jones win was assured.

The scooping action of the MacClain sand wedge met with the disfavor of the R&A and USGA, and they outlawed its use in 1931. Late that same year, frustrated by his bunker play, Gene began working on his own design for a sand wedge. The inspiration for his design was aeronautically inspired. The exact moment he was hit with the idea is a little cloudy, as he changed his story several times—as he was wont to do to give a story a good spin. The version that is most noted today is that he came up with the idea during a pleasure flight piloted by his pal, Howard Hughes. Another account, a number of years before the Howard Hughes version, was that Gene was at the Roosevelt Air Field on Long Island, waiting for a flight and observing a number of planes taking off. Gene became intrigued by the action of the flaps on a plane's tail during takeoff, and began to ponder the prospects of designing a club that would use the same principle to lift a ball out of a sand trap.

Soon after, Gene went to work on his idea while he was spending the winter in south Florida. He was staying in a rented bungalow on a nine-hole course in Port Richey. The course was far from first rate. It had only one decent sand trap, but it happened to be just a few paces from the back door of Gene's bungalow and became the test lab for Gene's idea. He had the Wilson Company send him 12 niblicks. Once the clubs arrived, he went to a local machine shop and began adjusting the angle and soldering extra lead to their soles. After long hours in the machine shop and in the test bunker, Gene's idea became a functioning reality.

Given the past history of the R&A's reluctance in embracing American ingenuity in club design, Gene decided that at the British Open he would keep his sand iron under wraps as much as possible and would instruct his caddie to keep the club blade down in his bag. Gene was planning for that caddie to be Skip Daniels. Since Daniels didn't travel from his hometown of Sandwich, he had not been available to Gene in his last three Open Championship appearances.

After his arrival in England, Gene spent several days in the London area. He played a round at Stokes Park, the noted resort course that would decades later be the scene of the filming of the golf match between Goldfinger and James Bond. At Stokes Park, Gene used the services of a firebrand young caddie. The two worked well together, as Gene shot a stellar round of five-under-par 67 on a course he had not laid eyes on before.

After the round, the caddie made a play to be Gene's caddie at the Open Championship. Gene advised him that he was planning to use Skip Daniels. The caddie was well aware of who Daniels was, and told Gene how much respect Daniels had in the caddie community. The caddie then called Daniels's health into question, saying he had heard that Daniels, now age 65, was not doing well.

Daniels had been far from a picture of health when he had caddied for Gene at Royal St. George's, so this gave him pause. After a few moments to think about it, he decided to go with the young caddie.

A few days later, Gene made the 75-mile trip down to Sandwich to begin his practice round for the Open Championship. When he stepped out of his car, he found Daniels waiting for him, eager to grab his bag. One look at Daniels and Gene was more than comfortable that he had made the right decision. Gene let Daniels down as easily as he could. Although Gene could tell how devastating the news was to him by his body language, Daniels's words in response to Gene's decision were very gracious. Recalling that moment in his book, *Thirty Years of Championship Golf*, Gene wrote:

> I had dreaded the thought of having to turn old Skip down, but I had never imagined that the scene would leave me reproaching myself as the biggest heel in the world. I attempted to justify what I had done by reminding myself that business was business and I couldn't afford to let personal feeling interfere with my determination to win the British Open. It didn't help much.

Gene began his practice rounds in earnest but soon found he had a big problem. The almost instant chemistry he had developed with his new caddie at Stokes Park was gone. They were now an oil-and-water duo, and Gene's practice rounds were painful to watch. To make matters worse, limping along in his gallery for those rounds was Skip Daniels.

A few days before the Open was to begin, Gene received a visit in his hotel room from one of Prince's more noted members. He was acting as an intermediary and brought a message from Skip Daniels. The member conveyed that it was clear to Daniels that Gene and his caddie were not getting along, and that Gene's play was suffering as a result. Skip believed he could get Gene back on track, if he would give him his bag.

Gene made the decision to switch back to Skip in a millisecond and the two began what would be a march to Gene's first and only British Open victory. It was a slow and arduous march for Skip. He had to use a cane to assist him in getting around the 7,000-yard course. All facets of Gene's game, from driving to putting to his sand play with his undercover sand wedge, were solid as a rock. He won in a runaway with a five-stroke margin of victory. His winning total of 283 was a record, besting by two strokes the mark set by Bobby Jones in 1925 at St. Andrews.

One feature of the British Open at that time was the bedlam that would break out on the 18th green after the winner had holed out. Like Hagen and Jones before him, Gene was being almost crushed by a jubilant throng of well-wishers. He had to inch his way toward the clubhouse until a member of the British Parliament came to his rescue. This individual was an atypical member of Parliament because of gender and birthplace. Clearing the way for Gene was Danville, Virginia, native and the first woman to serve in the Crown's governing body, Lady Astor. The former Nancy Witcher Langhorne, she had relocated to England after a failed first marriage and subsequently married another transplant from one of the richest American families: Waldorf Astor. Lady Astor was a golf enthusiast of the first order and had often teed up against her male colleagues in Parliament's annual match play tournament, and several times had advanced deep into the competition. On one of those occasions she made it as far as the semifinals before falling to a non-member of the body who had been given a royal exemption to participate in the event— the Prince of Wales.

With Lady Astor clearing the way, Gene was soon in the clubhouse. In the mayhem after his final putt, he had become separated from Skip. He asked officials to locate him so he could stand by him during the awards ceremony that was to take place on the clubhouse's balcony. Citing tradition, the officials declined Gene's request. That would be one of the two lingering regrets that Gene would have from his British Open victory; the other was the fact the Mary was not there with him to share the experience.

When he stepped out onto the balcony for the ceremony, Gene scanned the crowd looking for Skip and after several scans he finally saw him. He wasn't in the crowd below the balcony. He was riding his bike up the club's drive with a grandson on each handle bar. Skip had taken advantage of the time between the last putt and the ceremony to go home and get the lads so they could see Gene be awarded the cup.

A few days later, Gene and Skip shared their heartfelt goodbyes in front of the Prince's clubhouse. Several months later, Gene would receive word from an acquaintance in Sandwich that Skip had passed away.

Gene's arrival back in New York City didn't measure up to the bands that were playing for Walter Hagen in 1922 or the ticker-tape parade for Bobby Jones after his first British Open win in 1926, and again in 1930 after he won both the Open Championship and the British Amateur. But it was respectable. Gene was given the key to the city by Mayor Jimmy Walker and feted at a dinner at the Hotel Roosevelt that was attended by 600 people. In his remarks to the gathering, Gene let be known that he was excited about his chances of equaling Bobby Jones's feat of winning both Open Championships in the same year.

Gene didn't have long to wait for that opportunity. The first round of the U.S. Open was only six days away. You had to like Gene's chances. The Open was being held in the New York City area. He would be sleeping in his own bed each night, and it was being contested at the Fresh Meadow Golf Club, a course that until only recently he had served as head professional for six years.

Gene survived an up-and-down first round. The down was caused by some errant driving and deep rough that resulted in two double bogeys on par fours. The up was his putting, which bailed him out several times when he holed lengthy par savers. When the day was done, he was five strokes off the lead held by the long-hitting Olin Dutra.

When day two ended, Gene was still five strokes off the lead. Dutra had fallen deep back into the pack with a performance eight strokes higher than day one. The lead was now being shared by José Jurado, the Argentine who had had several strong recent performances in the British Open, and Philip Perkins, a former British Amateur champion who had turned professional three weeks earlier. He owed his coshare of the lead to his chipping and putting, as for the second straight day he had avoided a three-putt.

A native Brit, Perkins had relocated to the United States in 1929 and had been a regular in the country's big amateur events. In one of his last amateur appearances several months before the U.S. Open, the Dixie Amateur in Miami, Perkins had reached the finals of the match play event but then had to forfeit the match for a unique reason—he had suffered a gunshot wound.

The evening before that scheduled final, Perkins had been at one of Miami's hottest nightclubs. Shortly before midnight, six men brandishing pistols burst into the establishment, intent on robbing the club and its patrons. They herded the customers and employees up against a wall. In this herd were two plainclothes police officers who had been enjoying a complimentary meal at the club. A few moments after they had been lined up against the wall, the officers pulled out their weapons and opened fire. Mayhem ensued. One of the robbers grabbed Perkins and used him as a human shield. When the firing stopped, one robber was dead, three were wounded and in custody, and two had escaped. Perkins was one of several patrons who had been wounded. He was shot in the thigh, but made a complete recovery.

As usual, the first two rounds of the Open had been 18 holes, and the third and last day was a 36-hole affair. Before the start of round one, Gene had decided that he would adopt a conservative style of play. It appeared that all the goings-on of the last month, along with this conservative play, had produced a very stale game. As he left the eighth green during his morning 18 on that third and final day and headed for the tee of the ninth, he was four over for his round and seven strokes out of the lead.

At that point, Gene decided it was time to chuck the conservative strategy and go all in. He also wanted to make some adjustments to his surroundings. On days one and two, Gene had garnered the lion's share of the gallery. On this day he had some defections to Phil Perkins, who was the current leader, but he still had a throng following his play. For security, he had two uniformed police officers escorting him. Informing them that he had come to the conclusion they were jinxes, Gene dismissed them at the par-three ninth tee.

Moments later, Gene put his tee shot 12 feet from the pin and then rolled in his putt for birdie. On the back nine, he started with four solid pars. Then he reeled off three straight birdies to get to even for the day.

He wrapped up his morning round with two more solid pars. When all the scores for the morning round were posted, Gene was right in the thick of it. Phil Perkins was still the leader. Tied for second, one stroke back, were Gene and Leo Diegel.

In the break between rounds, Gene sat down in the dining room at a table with the world's most famous golfer—Bobby Jones. As would be his practice until he began experiencing health problems in the late 1940s, Jones was always at the U.S. Open. He would arrive a week early and meet up with Grantland Rice, and the two would play the course. At Fresh Meadow, Jones had also joined Gene for one of his practice rounds.

As Jones and Gene were their having lunch, Perkins began his final round. The buzz around the clubhouse was that Perkins would crack under the pressure. That would prove not to be the case, as he seemed to thrive on it. His only slip-up of the round came at the 16th hole when he recorded his lone three-putt of the tournament.

At the final hole, Perkins stood over a seven-foot birdie that would give him an even par 70 for the round. He addressed his ball but then abruptly backed away. He had been distracted by the winding sound of a newsreel camera. Perkins asked the cameraman if he would mind turning off his camera. And if he did so, once he had holed out, Perkins would reenact the putt for him. The cameraman agreed to the arrangement.

Perkins readdressed his ball and then confidently rolled it in for his birdie. After a few moments of acknowledging the applause of the gallery, Perkins returned to the spot where he had putted from to do one for the camera. He made that one too.

The recent amateur-turned-professional was in with a score of one over par, and many around the green thought that he was going to be the winner. Then Bobby Cruickshank, the loser to Bobby Jones in an 18-hole play-off for U.S. Open title nine years earlier, came in a few groups later and matched Perkins's score. But the prospects for a play-off in 1932 were soon all but extinguished when word reached the clubhouse that Gene, at the halfway point of his back nine, was on fire.

Gene had matched the 32 he recorded on the back nine of the morning round with another 32 on the front side of his afternoon round. This six-under-par total for his last 18 holes had bolted him into a two-stroke lead. He expanded that lead by another stroke with a birdie early on his back nine. It would turn out that the only slip-up Gene would make on his final back nine would come at the 72nd and final hole. His approach shot flew over the pin and landed in a bunker at the back of the green.

Most of the throng of fans in attendance that day were now clustered around the green and down both sides of the fairway. After Gene's ball plopped in the bunker, all crowd-control measures broke down. Fans surged not around the green, but onto it.

It was proving almost impossible to get the crowd under control. Gene and his playing partner, Willie Klein, struggled to make it through the throng. Security had only cleared about a third of the green when Gene's patience expired and he decided to take out his trusty new sand iron and go ahead and play his shot.

Standing a few feet behind the bunker was a good friend of Gene's, Paul Gallico, the sports editor of the *New York Daily News*. Gallico would later become a noted novelist and short-story writer. His works would include the tearjerker *The Snow Goose* and *The Poseidon Adventure*, which later became a major hit on the silver screen. Gallico pleaded with Gene to wait for more of the green to be cleared, but Gene ignored his pleas. His blast from the sand stopped eight feet from the cup.

The crowd surged again and enveloped Gene, leaving him in a 20-foot circle. Gene wasted no time. He calmly rolled in the putt for an up and down par. It would be 28 years before another golfer bettered Gene's 66 in the final round of the U.S. Open—a 65 turned in at the 1960 U.S. Open at the Cherry Hills Golf Club in Denver by its winner, Arnold Palmer.

As soon as the putt had dropped, the crowd engulfed Gene. For a minute or two, he could make no headway in exiting the green. Fortunately for Gene, the two policemen he had summarily dismissed late that morning reappeared and cleared a path for him to the clubhouse. A half-hour later the awards ceremony took place on the lawn in front of the clubhouse in front of a half-dozen newsreel cameras and a microphone that was broadcasting the proceedings over a national radio network.

When he accepted the trophy and the winner's check of $1,000, the ultra-talkative Gene reverted to the way he had been at the Skokie ceremony in 1922, at a loss for words. With difficulty, he uttered a two-sentence thank you.

After his win at Fresh Meadow, Gene's focus turned to the last leg of what was for a golf professional the game's Triple Crown. Gene would be the first pro to have a shot at it. PGA officials were practically beside themselves with the attention the event was drawing as a result. Most likely in part to pay homage to Gene's two Open victories and perhaps to ensure the unthinkable wouldn't happen—Gene failing to qualify for the event—they offered him an exemption into the field. He turned it down. He wanted to have to qualify just like every other player.

The 36-hole qualifier for the Northeast section of the PGA took place at the Rockville Golf and Country Club on Long Island. One hundred and fourteen players were competing for 16 spots. Gene struggled throughout the morning and afternoon rounds; he needed a six-foot putt for par at the finishing hole to safely make the field. He missed it. All was not lost. His 36-hole total left him in a seven-way play-off for the last three spots. On the first play-off hole, three players birdied to make the field. Gene was not one of them.

History had repeated itself. When Gene had a shot at winning three major events in succession (but not in the same year) at the 1923 British Open at Troon, he had his most embarrassing moment in golf by failing to qualify. This failure at Rockville had to rate as his second most embarrassing moment. And to add insult to injury, his assistant at the Lakeville Country Club, Charles Lacey, made the field that day by two strokes.

Gene's failure to make the field was an even bigger blow to the PGA. Without the game's biggest name and draw, it had the feel of just another golf tournament. It took place at Keller Golf Course in Maplewood, Minnesota, a suburb of St. Paul. Olin Dutra was the winner.

Gene finished out 1932 by playing in a couple of tournaments and a host of exhibition matches in the New York City area and in the Midwest. In mid-December the Associated Press named him 1932 Athlete of the Year.

10

THE BIG CUP

During this era, January was not a month where one could usually find a lot of space on the nation's sports pages about golf. However, this was not the case in January 1933, as there was plenty of space being dedicated to golf and it was being driven by Bobby Jones and Gene Sarazen. The coverage of Jones took place in the first half of the month. It was not about his golf game but his golf creation: the Augusta National Golf Club. The coverage of Sarazen began in the middle of January and extended almost to the end of winter. And like Jones, his coverage was not about his game, but about an idea that he was espousing that would radically change one major aspect of golf.

Early in the second week of January, a special train departed New York City, after stops in Philadelphia and Washington, DC; approximately 100 passengers were on board. Among them were big-name sportswriters and captains of industry and finance who shared a common interest: an immense passion for the game of golf. The train's destination was Augusta, Georgia, and the passengers on board were to be Bobby Jones's guests at the grand opening of the Augusta National Golf Club.

Augusta, Georgia, was by no means a Johnny-come-lately to the game of golf. In the 1880s it became a favorite resort spot for affluent Northerners to escape the doldrums of winter. In 1889, Augusta achieved premier tourist-destination status with the opening of the 300 room, top-drawer Bon Air Hotel. As golf was beginning to take hold in the country, the hotel added a golf course several years later.

In 1903, just across the Savannah River in North Augusta, South Carolina, another exclusive hotel opened—the Hampton Terrace. It was five stories high and boasted over 300 rooms. Heralded as one of the finest hotels in the South, the cornerstone of its amenities was a golf course. Other features included a music auditorium for orchestra concerts and a grand ballroom. Besides golf, a wealth of other outdoor activities was available to the guests, among them horseback riding, tennis, and hunting.

The area's standing in golf was further enhanced when two of the country's biggest names and most passionate golfers began to make frequent trips to Augusta. The first on the scene was the country's richest man, John D. Rockefeller. He had taken up the game a decade earlier at the age of 57, after a friend had witnessed the smooth and fluid motion Mr. Rockefeller used when pitching horseshoes and suggested that the oil tycoon had the makings of a good golfer. Mr. Rockefeller's enthusiasm for the game was on par with his zeal for making a dollar. He had courses built on his estates in Cleveland and New York, and in the winter months he traveled to Florida to golf, frequently making stopovers in Augusta on the way down and on the way back.

The second individual in this powerful duo was William Howard Taft. In 1908, Theodore Roosevelt hand-picked the 51-year-old, his secretary of war, to be the Republican Party's nominee to succeed him as president. Roosevelt believed that Taft had all the tools necessary to keep the country on the right path, but recommended that Taft be careful about one aspect of his personal life. Since Taft weighed 340 pounds, you would have thought Roosevelt would have been concerned about Taft's girth. But weight wasn't what was weighing heavy on the president's mind about Taft. It was something that he considered far more politically dangerous than being morbidly obese—the game of golf.

Taft had been introduced to golf by his younger brother, Henry Waters Taft, a prominent New York City attorney and one of the early members of the St. Andrew's Golf Club in Yonkers.

Before Roosevelt had named him Secretary of War in 1904, Taft had served as a state judge, the U.S. solicitor general, a judge on the U.S. Court of Appeals and, through appointment by President McKinley, the governor-general of the Philippines. But he had never run for an elective office. On an early campaign swing through the Midwest, Taft created quite a stir when he took a few breaks to play golf. Mail began pouring in to the White House, critical of the preoccupation with the game by his hand-picked candidate. Roosevelt fired off a letter to Taft with a dire warning about his golf. He wrote:

> I have received literally hundreds of letters from the West protesting about it. I myself play tennis, but that game is a little more familiar; besides, you never saw a photograph of me playing tennis; photographs on horseback, yes; tennis no. And golf is fatal.

Taft chose to ignore the president's advice and even turned up the focus on his golf, bringing up his interest in the game during gatherings at campaign stops. Taft went on to handily defeat his Democratic opponent, William Jennings Bryan.

Up until the first inauguration of Franklin Delano Roosevelt in 1933, presidents took the oath of office in early March. Taft took advantage of the extended period between his election and his inauguration to take a nearly six-week working vacation in Augusta. In the mornings, he worked on matters concerning his upcoming presidency and during the afternoons, he golfed almost every day.

In early January, John D. Rockefeller made a stopover in Augusta on his way to wintering in Florida. Shortly after his arrival, he sent an invitation to President-elect Taft to join him for a round of golf.

Taft was amenable to the invitation, but Mrs. Taft vetoed the idea. Despite the fact he had just won election to the presidency, his spouse's political instincts were much keener than his in this instance. During the building of his financial empire, Rockefeller had forged quite the negative image for his business practices. While he was the country's richest man, he was also in the top tier of the nation's most unpopular individuals, especially among the country's rank and file. Mrs. Taft knew the press reports of her husband on the course with Rockefeller would trigger a firestorm of negative public opinion.

Rockefeller was more than a little miffed by the snub. Later, he did extract a measure of payback. Taft continued to make trips to Augusta throughout his four years as president, and on one of those occasions he made the decision to go there on short notice. When he and his entourage arrived at the Bon Air Hotel, they found the hotel short of the number of rooms they would need. As it turned out, Rockefeller was in town and also staying at the Bon Air. As was his custom, Rockefeller had booked a large block of rooms, and it was known to the hotel staff that many of these rooms were unoccupied.

The management of the Bon Air contacted Mr. Rockefeller and asked him if he might give up a few of his rooms so they could accommodate the party of the president of the United States. Rockefeller declined.

Augusta reached its peak as a winter golf resort in 1927 with the opening of the Forrest Hills-Ricker Hotel. Built at a cost of $2 million, the Forrest Hills-Ricker boasted a $100,000 golf course designed by Donald Ross. The course's first and tenth tees, as well as the ninth and eighteenth greens, were practically at the hotel's front door. Ads touting the new course proclaimed it offered "the finest winter golf in America."

The stock market crash and the Depression that followed was a blow that sent Augusta as a popular winter resort for many into the doldrums. It would never again achieve the scale that it had enjoyed for four decades. But what it would lose in quantity, it would soon regain in unmatched quality with the opening of Bobby Jones's dream course.

In 1929, the U.S. Amateur was held at the Pebble Beach Golf Links on California's Monterey Peninsula. Having won the event four of the last five times it was held, it was almost a forgone conclusion that Bobby Jones would take the event. When playing his second practice round at Pebble Beach, Jones solidified those expectations, setting a new course record with a five-under-par 67.

But in the first round of Amateur, it was like an earthquake had rocked the Monterey Peninsula. The mighty Jones fell to a 19-year-old former caddie from Nebraska, Johnny Goodman, in a match that was not decided until the final hole. In the gallery of almost 2,000 that had followed the contest, there was almost as much gloom over the unexpected downfall Jones had suffered as there was enthusiastic appreciation for the astonishing feat of young Goodman.

But every dark cloud has a silver lining; Jones's defeat would benefit the design of his dream course four years later. The day after his defeat at the hands of Goodman, Jones was afforded the opportunity to do something that he would not have had the time to do had he advanced in the Amateur. He traveled a few miles down the road and played one of the most talked-about courses in the country—Cypress Point.

Jones found the course more than lived up to the buzz he had heard. He was enormously impressed with the way the architect, Dr. Alister MacKenzie, had laid out the course. Subsequently, the two men had the occasion to meet and found their ideas and thoughts on golf course design were finely in tune. When it came time to pick an architect for Augusta National, Jones chose MacKenzie.

MacKenzie's route to becoming one of golf's foremost course architects was a unique one. He was initially in the medical profession as a surgeon. He took up golf in his early 20s. In 1900, when he was in his late 20s, MacKenzie worked as a civilian surgeon for the British army during the second Boer War waged between the British and the Dutch settlers in South Africa. The Dutch in South Africa were known as the Boers, and were vastly outnumbered by the British, so the Boer commanders decided to adopt a guerrilla style of warfare. The British eventually prevailed in the conflict.

MacKenzie had been intrigued by the effectiveness of the camouflage techniques the Boers had used. Soon after his return to Great Britain, he began to dabble in golf course design and incorporated a great deal of camouflaging technique into those designs. When Britain entered World War I, MacKenzie served in the British army—not as a surgeon, but as an artillery officer. In this capacity, he continued to study the art of camouflage.

After World War I, MacKenzie left medicine at the age of 49 to pursue a second career as a full-time golf course architect. Fourteen years later, when he arrived in Augusta to begin work on Augusta National, he had designed over 40 courses on four continents. The most noted beside Cypress Point were the West Course at Royal Melbourne in Australia; Pasatiempo Golf Club in Santa Cruz, California; and the Old Course at Lahinch Golf Club in Ireland.

When Jones and MacKenzie finished their collaboration in Augusta, they had constructed what many called the most subtle golf course in the country. Augusta National featured wide fairways and no real rough to speak of. By the standards of the day, it had very few sand traps. The greens seemed to be welcoming one's approach shot with open arms.

In keeping with MacKenzie's keenness for camouflage, the greens were an ambush. One slight slip-up and the player could find himself in a very bad way. If he was long, he could face a treacherous downhill chip or long putt. If he was short, he encountered tricky little mounds and aprons that seemed to vary in consistency from one hole to the other. Most players were accustomed to encountering this type of a situation at a few holes during a round, but the task at Augusta was withstanding it for all 18. Throughout the years after Augusta National was opened, when Jones was complimented on the course, he would always be quick to point out that MacKenzie was the architect and that he had been the advisor and consultant.

Friday the 13th of January 1933 was the official opening day for the Augusta National Golf Club. Jones opted not to play that day, choosing to devote his time to catering to the needs of his guests. He did play on the second day. He made five birdies and shot a 69.

Two weeks after the Augusta National opening, Jones headed back to Hollywood to make a series of short golf instructional films. One in particular was titled *How to Break Ninety*. Gene was also in the Hollywood area and he had been there for almost a month. As mentioned earlier, Gene's reputation as a publicity hound was well-earned. His skill at grabbing press attention was second only to his golf game.

Two days before the opening of the course where he would in a few years hit the most famous shot in golf history, Gene pulled off his biggest publicity grab ever. Like his unforgettable shot at Augusta, it would be pulled off from a difficult lie—a hospital bed in Santa Monica, California.

Gene had made the three-day trip from the East Coast shortly after New Year's Day, arriving just in time to play in the LA Open. After two rounds, he was forced to withdraw because he wasn't feeling well. The next day, he checked into a nearby hospital in Santa Monica, where it was determined he had the flu.

A few days later, he granted an interview to an Associated Press reporter from his hospital bed. In the interview that ran in papers nationwide, Gene declared that golf "had gotten too tame" and he had just the idea to give it some new energy. His brainchild was to widen the cup from its current width of four and a quarter inches to eight. With the hole almost doubled in size, he was sure the weekend golfer's enjoyment of the game would increase by leaps and bounds, and for professional tournaments he was of the opinion that it would become commonplace for the pros to post scores in the 60s in all four rounds of a tournament.

Had this proposal been brought forward by anyone but the defending U.S. Open and British Open champion, it is unlikely it would have gotten off the ground. But because it was Gene Sarazen, it did. And for a publicity hound like Gene, it was manna from heaven and more, as it was a story that would keep his name in the forefront of the press for almost six weeks.

A few days after the interview was published, Gene's voice was reduced to a whisper as his doctors decided that his tonsils had to go, but his eight-inch cup idea was making an abundance of noise, both pro and con.

On the plus side, a course in Kansas City found it had a set of posthole diggers with the exact width that was needed, and turned its back nine into a testing ground for the eight-inch cup. A host of the club's players participated in the test and most were very positive about the idea, as many believed the enlarged cups had lowered their score for those nine holes by two to three strokes.

On the negative side, and on the same day as the Kansas City test, another trial of the idea took place at one of golf's most prestigious locales, Pinehurst No. 2 in Pinehurst, North Carolina. Taking part in the test were several prominent names in the game of golf: famed golf course designer Donald Ross; Richard S. Tufts, the son of the founder of Pinehurst Golf Resort and its current director and a future USGA president; and William Clark Fownes Jr., the principal owner of the Oakmont Country Club, a former U.S. Amateur champion and a former USGA president. This group was the polar opposite of the Kansas City group. After their trial, they were all thumbs down.

Among Sarazen's tournament-playing contemporaries, support for the idea was in the 30–35 percent category. Opposition in the remaining 65–70 percent ranged from lukewarm to heartily against. The *New York Times* reported that when asked for his opinion, Albert R. Gates, administrator for the PGA, refused to give any credence to the idea. He said, "I think Gene is kidding the public a bit."

Where Gene's proposal seemed to really strike a nerve was among the elder statesmen of the game in Great Britain. Six-time British Open Champion Harry Vardon called Gene's idea "Tommyrot!" Sandy Herd, winner of the 1902 British Open, deemed Gene's idea "farcical." He declared, "You would have to be blind to miss an eight-inch cup."

The criticism of his idea did not sit well with Gene. Still in the hospital, he put in a call, which would be chronicled the next day in the *Los Angeles Times*, to the Associated Press office in Los Angeles. When a reporter answered the phone, the conversation with Gene went like this:

"This is Sarazen in rebuttal."

"In what?"

"Rebuttal. It is a legal word means a comeback. Sort of a counter-punch."

"What do you propose to rebut?"

"Some of my friends who are firing at me for my suggestion that the golf cups be increased to eight inches. From the papers some of them seem to think I'm loony."

"Go ahead."

"Well, take the British. I see I can't get any support there. Well, I am not surprised for I did not expect my friends on the other side would agree with me in any proposal for a change in the game of golf. My answer to that is that in the old days we fought with knives and swords and now we fight with airplanes.

"A lot of games have been better for changes. In baseball, once upon a time a batter was out if a fielder caught a ball on the first bounce but not anymore.

"I noticed Pinehurst didn't think much of the big cup. The answer to that is they have sand greens there. A 12-inch cup wouldn't make any difference on a sand green."

In response to Mr. Gates, the administrator of the PGA, Gene said this: "Mr. Gates thinks I am kidding the public. I am not kidding anybody."

Gene welcomed all the tests that were being scheduled by clubs across the country. But he believed the real test would come when the cups were used by professionals in the 72-hole tournament in Miami he was planning for the first week in March.

The day after his call to the Associated Press, Gene was released from the hospital and traveled back to Miami. Meanwhile, tests were continuing across the country.

Within a few days of arriving in Miami, Gene was out on the practice green, putting at an eight-inch cup. After several days of practice, he concluded that an eight-inch cup was just a little too large, that a six-inch cup was the way to go, and that the six-inch size would be used in the upcoming enlarged cup tournament.

Before that tournament, Gene had a commitment to play in a match with the standard cup size. Since his match with Walter Hagen back in 1922 for the title of "Unofficial World Champion," there had been almost a yearly rendition in some form or another, and this year was no exception. As the winner of both Open Championships, he was set to play Olin Dutra, who had won the PGA Championship that Gene had missed when he failed to qualify in Miami.

In his match against Olin, played at the Miami-Biltmore course, Gene showed no ill effects from his long layoff. The match was 72 holes over two days. On day one, Gene, thanks to a red-hot putter, put together rounds of 68 and 67. At the end of the day he held a commanding seven-up lead. Day two was a short one. Gene closed out the match at the 27th hole, when he went ten-up with nine to play.

A week later, with six-inch cups in place, the Miami-Biltmore hosted what was called "The Florida Year Round Club $5,000 Open." Its field of 102 included almost all of the big-name players. After the end of day one, the scores were good but not the super-low scores that many were expecting. Al Espinosa and Willie McFarlane shared the lead at four-under-par 67. Gene, who had putted so well in his match the prior week with the standard cup, struggled with the bigger target and shot 76.

On day two, the scores overall ticked a little higher, except for the card turned in by Paul Runyan. He was on a bit of a hot streak. He had won the Agua Caliente during the West Coast swing and had recently taken a Florida event as well. Runyan, like Sarazen, was short in stature; his nickname was "Little Poison." He was considered one of the game's best putters and the best player with pitches and chips. He shot a seven-under-par 64 to take a one-shot lead. The high point of his round came when he holed an 80-yard shot.

Rounds three and four were played on the last day of the tournament. Again, the only player who excelled was Paul. He posted rounds of 65 and 68 to take the event by 10 strokes. Except for Paul, no one else in field had made any noise with their putting. Gene had rallied over the last 36 holes with rounds of 67 and 68. But he had scored just as well on that course the week before against Olin Dutra with the standard size cup.

Scores were considered to be one to two strokes better per round, but the excitement Gene contended would come with the larger cups never materialized.

In interviews with the participants after the tournament, it became clear that the pros did not care for the enlarged cups. The best putters among them had the most problems. They found it difficult to find a central spot of focus on such a large target. Gene tried to put a different spin on the situation. He argued that a single tournament was not a fair test, that three or four would be needed. That was not going to happen, and the idea seemed to die with the same speed that it had caught fire when he had first proposed it six weeks earlier.

Although the enlarged cup idea failed, it was a big success in terms of what a number of prominent members of the press considered the main objective: to keep Gene's name in the forefront on the sports page. Two of the nation's top sportswriters were less than impressed with Gene in this regard—one commented with tongue in cheek, and the other was direct and to the point.

The tongue-in-cheek writer was John Kieran of the *New York Times*. Two decades earlier he had been pulled out of the cub reporter pool and dispatched to cover a golf tournament. The quality of that coverage propelled his writing career on a rapid upward trajectory. A dozen years later, he became the first reporter in the history of the *New York Times* to have a bylined column. Kieran named his column "Sports of the Times." When Kieran ended his long run at the *Times*, his column was handed off to Red Smith and, later, to Dave Anderson.

During the six-week life of Gene's enlarged cup story, Kieran wrote about it in his "Sports of the Times" column. Kieran theorized that Gene had concocted the idea while in a hospital bed and could have been "possibly delirious." On another occasion, he referenced Gene's publicity-hound traits with this comment, "Jolly Gene Sarazen. . . . He is always doing something to attract attention."

The direct-and-to-the-point sportswriter was a native of Bar Harbor, Maine, a popular summer resort. His last name was Povich. At his birth his parents chose a name for their newborn son that was very popular in their area—Shirley. Like Kieran at the *New York Times,* Shirley Povich's big break in the newspaper business came because of golf. When he was in his teens, he spent his summers caddying at the Kebo Valley Golf Club. One day Shirley had the good fortune to carry the bag for a golf fanatic from Washington, DC. The bag belonged Ned McLean, the owner of the *Washington Post*. McLean found Shirley to be an excellent caddie and retained his services during his lengthy stay that summer and the following summer as well.

Soon after high school graduation, Povich found his way to the Washington, DC, area and the doorstep of McLean's estate. That very afternoon, he was caddying on McLean's private golf course in a foursome that included President Warren G. Harding.

The next day, Povich began work as a copy boy for the *Washington Post*, making $12 a week. He picked up an extra $20 each week by caddying for McLean on Sundays. Povich made a rapid rise through the ranks at the *Post* and at just 24 years of age, he was named the paper's sports editor.

In his almost decade-long tenure as sports editor, Povich earned the reputation as one of the profession's straightest shooters. The year before he had been skeptical about Sarazen's effort at self-promotion when he trumpeted that he had insured his hands for $100,000 and that a new agent, despite the still Depression-staggered economy, was guaranteeing him an income of $250,000 from endorsements and promotions. Povich had also been critical of Sarazen missing the PGA Championship the year before, expressing the opinion that the golfer's bravado prevented him from accepting the exemption that the PGA had offered.

At the beginning of the eight-inch-cup campaign, Povich declared that the only thing giving the idea any credence was that it was being championed by the defending British Open and U.S. Open champion. When Gene fell back from the eight inches to six, it struck a nerve with Povich. He lambasted Gene because he was of the opinion the Gene had done a disservice to those who had jumped on his bandwagon at the outset for the eight-inch cup, leaving them in the lurch.

Several days after the six-inch-cup tournament, Gene caught some heavy flak from Westbrook Pegler, another prominent member of the press. Pegler had started his journalistic career covering World War I on the front lines. After the war, he covered sports for almost a decade before becoming a very successful general-interest columnist who was syndicated in over 100 newspapers. Pegler was a champion of the working man, and for him no story or individual was out of bounds. He would later win a Pulitzer Prize for his coverage of corruption in labor unions. If you were the target of a Pegler column, you were said to have been "Peglerized."

Pegler had a love-hate relationship with golf. He loved the game but hated the way he played it, as he rarely broke 100. He followed the game with great interest.

Throughout the run of the enlarged cup story, Gene had also been espousing his views on a number of topics pertaining to the game. He believed that only 200 golfers in a million had their hands on the club correctly. Giving no regard to his own pedigree as a caddie and apparently forgetting Skip Daniels's contribution to his win in the British Open, Gene declared that the dumber the caddie the better, because a player needed to rely on his own judgment in club selection and reading greens.

Another issue that Gene discussed was golfer attire and, in this instance as well, he appeared to have a lapse of memory. In an interview with a United Press reporter, Gene declared, in a way that the interviewer described as almost violent, that golfers were "dressing the game not playing it." A silk shirt, a kerchief, and cravat were becoming the fashion of the day at the first tee. This was all wrong. According to Gene, "golfers should dress conservatively."

Gene's comments on this subject really set Pegler off, since he considered Sarazen, with good reason, to have been one of the prime standard bearers for flashy golf fashion for a decade. In a 950-word column in the *Chicago Tribune* he devoted two-thirds of it to taking on Sarazen over his double standard: "Hey, Mr. Sarazen! Where's Your Memory." Pegler went into great detail about Gene's passion for fashion on the course, as well of that of Walter Hagen and Johnny Farrell. Pegler was of the opinion that, when Sarazen and Farrell left the locker room for the first tee, they were under the impression they were in a Mr. America competition. Pegler also made mention of the fact that among their rivals, Sarazen and Farrell were often referred to as the "Dolly Sisters."

11

IN THE SAND AT ST. ANDREWS

For several weeks after the six-inch-cup tournament, Gene kept a low profile. There were a few clubs around the country that were continuing to test the idea, but with the movement's advocate now quiet, it faded away with the same high speed it featured at its birth.

In early April the team for the 1933 Ryder Cup was announced. Of course, Gene was on the team along with Walter Hagen—who was again named captain—and Olin Dutra, Horton Smith, Leo Diegel, and Paul Runyan were the other big names. Three others of lesser note, Craig Wood, Ed Dudley, and Denny Shute, made up the nine that were chosen by ballots submitted by the 25 PGA sections across the country. A 10th spot on the team was being held open for the 1933 U.S. Open winner, provided he was not in the nine already selected and was a home-bred, which, despite Hagen's efforts against this requirement, was still a stipulation.

This was the first time this particular selection process was used, and the PGA had hoped the results would be met with peace and harmony by its members. That hope was abruptly jolted when Gene hit the ceiling because Billy Burke, a player he believed ranked as the fifth or sixth best professional in country, had been left off the team. Burke had been the star of the 1931 Ryder Cup, won the 1931 U.S. Open, and had finished sixth in the 1932 Open. Gene believed Burke's resume far exceeded several of the other nine selections, and his stance on the matter received an abundance of attention in the press.

The next day, Tommy Armour joined Gene in decrying the omission of Burke from the team. In an Associated Press story with a Chicago dateline that ran in the *Washington Post*, Armour called the matter "one of the outstanding disgraces of golf." Like Gene, he put a lot of weight on Burke's performance in big events and decried the accomplishments of some of those who had made the team, stating, "Any golfer can come along and win a few tournaments on the winter circuit but where are they when the big show is on? Nowhere!"

Despite the outcries of Gene, Armour, and several others, the PGA, which initially seemed to have been set back on its heels by the criticism, held its ground. It was buoyed by the fact that Hagen had come to its defense by stating he was in agreement with the results of the selection process.

Gene had plenty of time to voice his displeasure on the subject because he was taking several weeks off from playing golf. He was resting up for a golf marathon that would see him play 30 exhibition matches in 30 days. The marathon would begin in Georgia and conclude in Massachusetts. Accompanying Gene on the tour as his playing partner would be Joe Kirkwood.

Born in Sidney, Australia, Joe Kirkwood was the player who put Australian golf on the world map. Having been introduced to the game when he was 10 by a sheep farmer, Kirkwood won the Australian Open and the New Zealand Open in 1920 when he was 23, the latter by a record 12 strokes. The following year, he played in the British Open and captured sixth place.

After the 1921 British Open, Kirkwood came to the United States to compete in a number of tournaments and created quite a stir with another aspect of his golf ability—that of a trick-shot artist. In this regard, Kirkwood was one of the best the game has ever known. He typically performed his trick-shot routine before exhibition matches. His signature stunt was to drive a golf ball teed up on a gold watch that was resting on top of the shoe of a very trusting friend or volunteer.

Early in 1922, Kirkwood was offered the guaranteed sum of $12,000 to become the head professional at a new club outside of Washington, DC. This amount was believed to be the highest salary ever offered a pro in the United States for a club position.

Kirkwood turned the offer down. His extended stay in the United States was being underwritten by a pool of Australian golfers who wanted him to represent their country in competitions and exhibitions across the States during the 1922 golf season. Kirkwood felt duty bound to honor that commitment. But when Kirkwood entered the 1923 British Open, he listed his country as the United States. He had become Americanized. When asked about the switch, Kirkwood stated his reason: "The finest golfers and sportsmen in the world are in the United States."

Gene and Joe Kirkwood would be traveling in style on their tour in a Curtis Aero car, a forerunner to today's recreational vehicles, and it was outfitted with all of the day's most modern appointments. The car was provided by Colonel Henry L. Dougherty, the owner of the Miami-Biltmore Hotel and Golf Club. Gene was using the tour to get into shape to defend both of his Open titles and for his play in the Ryder Cup. The golf calendar of the big events in 1933 was far from player friendly. The U.S. Open was scheduled in the Chicago area from June 8 to 11. The Ryder Cup team would sail for England at midnight on June 14. Their ship would arrive in England on June 21. The Ryder Cup would take place three days later at the Ainsdale Golf Club in Southport. At its conclusion, the players would head to St. Andrews for British Open qualifying, which would begin on July 3. Those that qualified would begin play in the Open Championship on July 5.

Gene had been enjoying the good life since his two Open wins in 1932 and had picked up about 10 pounds. On the day the tour kicked off, the *Washington Post* reported that Gene was asked what his diet would be on his 30-day "get in shape tour." He replied, "It is going to be beer and vegetables and fruit."

Once the tour began, Gene received an abundance of press attention at each stop. In these interviews he continued his rant over the Billy Burke matter, and he appeared to be giving off the vibe that he was disappointed that he was not selected captain of the Ryder Cup team. At one stop, he espoused that no one should hold that position more than once. Hagen would now be serving in that post for the fourth time. Before an exhibition in Washington, DC, Gene expressed the belief that he was going to successfully defend both of his Open titles.

Sarazen and Kirkwood's tour ended two weeks before the U.S. Open. It was being held at the North Shore Country Club in Glenview, Illinois. Gene arrived several days in advance of the event. But unfortunately his game never showed up, as he appeared to have golfed himself out on his 30-stop tour. On day one, he was six shots off the pace. On day two, he was 10 shots behind. The final 36 holes were played on day three, and it was almost painful to watch the defending champion struggle. When all was said and done, Gene finished in 26th place, 15 strokes behind the winner.

In his autobiography, *The Walter Hagen Story*, Hagen recalled that during the run-up to the Open, Gene had gotten a little lippy about his chances, telling reporters that Walter was "too old and feeble to play any longer with the brisk young fellows and should be seated somewhere in the shade in a comfortable chair."

Walter, playing well ahead of Gene in the final round, posted a score that gave him a fourth-place finish. He had been more than a little ticked over Gene's comfortable chair comments and took full advantage of the moment. He paid a locker room attendant handsomely to take a chair out to the 17th green and to present it to Gene as he exited the green, with Walter's compliments.

With the winner of the Open, golf had its feel-good story of the year. It was amateur Johnny Goodman from Omaha, Nebraska, the same Johnny Goodman who had beaten Bobby Jones in the first round of the 1929 U.S. Amateur. Goodman, the youngest of 13 children, was orphaned at age 11 and began caddying at age 12. By his late teens, he had developed quite the game. He earned the nickname the "Hobo Kid" because in his early days on the amateur circuit, he often sneaked onto freight trains to travel to tournaments.

Goodman grabbed the lead in the Open with a 66 in the second round and held onto it the rest of the away, surviving a late charge by Ralph Guldahl, who missed a birdie attempt at the final hole that would have forced a play-off.

Since Goodman was an amateur, he was ineligible for the Ryder Cup team. This left the PGA in a quandary, since it was hoping to fill the final spot with the U.S. Open winner. One would have thought the PGA would give the spot to Guldahl, since he was the highest finishing professional in the field. But it chose Billy Burke, even though he had made a poor showing in the Open, finishing 33rd. One would suspect the reason was Gene's outcries on Burke's behalf.

From Chicago the Ryder Cup members traveled to New York City. Three days later, a couple of hours after a dinner in their honor, the players boarded the cruise liner *Aquitania* shortly before midnight for the six-day journey to England. Each member of the team had been given $1,000 to cover his expenses.

The Ryder Cup took place on the Irish Sea coast of Northwest England, at the Ainsdale Golf Club in Southport. As in the three previous Ryder Cups, the format consisted of four foursome matches on the first day and eight singles matches on the second day, for a total of 12 points. Therefore, six and a half points were required to win the Cup. All matches were scheduled for 36 holes.

In the foursomes the first day, Walter chose to be paired with Gene. Their pairing had not occurred in the three previous Ryder Cups. They were the first out of the four matches, and the two did not have their best day. They were four down after the morning 18. In the afternoon session, they pulled even and finished that way, thanks to their opponents, Percy Alliss and Charles Whitcombe, each losing a hole by missing a two-foot putt. Matches two and three were won by the British. The United States appeared on the verge of going winless on the first day, but Billy Burke's clutch putting saved the day and gave him and his partner, Ed Dudley, a one-up victory over Alf Padgham and Alf Perry.

Trailing two and a half to one and a half after day one meant the Americans would have to win five of the eight matches on day two to retain the cup. Surprisingly, despite the fact that he had been the U.S. star on the final day of the 1931 Ryder Cup and the first day of the 1933 edition, Hagen chose to sit Burke on the final day.

The final day's play took place on a Tuesday. Despite being a weekday, the finals drew what Bernard Darwin, who by this point had been covering golf in Great Britain for over a quarter-century, characterized as the largest gallery he had ever witnessed at a golf event. Estimates placed the number at 10,000-plus, and they were a raucous bunch.

Hagen sent Gene out in the first match. He got the Americans off to a good start with a six-up with four to play win over Padgham. The U.S. team dropped the second match, but won three and four to put the pressure on. The outcome was not decided until the last match on the course, when Syd Easterbrook and Denny Shute reached the final hole and Easterbrook prevailed to give the British a six and a half to five and a half victory.

The British capturing the Ryder Cup spurred the hope that in just a few days there would be a British subject hoisting the Claret Jug at the conclusion of the Open Championship at St. Andrews. Of the last 10

British Opens, home-bred Americans had won eight and transplants from Great Britain who were living in the States had won the other two.

The 1933 British Open marked the 14th time the event had been held at the Old Course at St. Andrews, but there was a big change from the previous 13 that had the townspeople of St. Andrews agitated. For the first time in the roughly 500-year history of their beloved golf layout, they were going to be required to pay an admission charge of a half-crown (54 cents American) to access it.

This would be the first time that Gene had ever played the Old Course at St. Andrews. It hosted the Open Championship every six years, and its most recent was in 1921, two years prior to Gene's first trip over for a British Open, and again in 1927, one of the four years since 1923 that Gene did not make the trip. After several practice rounds, he sent a note to Dave Herman, the golf writer at the *Washington Post*. In it he wrote, "They say it is old-fashioned but I am telling you it is the most artistic golf course in the world."

The Old Course at that time was playing to a par 73. Gene qualified in the middle of the pack with a 36-hole score of two over. In the opening round, he was one of 25 golfers to post a score under par in the 117-man field with a one-under 72. This placed him four strokes behind the leader, his old nemesis Walter Hagen. Carrying over his strong play from the U.S. Open, Walter shot a brilliant 68, which gave him a two-stroke lead.

On day two, Gene made a strong push to catch up with Hagen. Heading for the par three 11th tee, he was two under for the day and three under for the tournament.

Both Bobby Jones and Alister MacKenzie had a deep admiration for the Old Course at St. Andrews, and when they designed the Augusta National course a strong connection between no fewer than six holes at St. Andrews could be seen in the Augusta National layout. The strongest connection of these six is between the 11th hole at the Old Course and the fourth hole at Augusta National. The location of the bunkers and tilt of the green were acknowledged by both MacKenzie and Jones as having been designed and placed with the 11th at St. Andrews in mind.

Eden, as the 11th hole at the Old Course is named, played at 164 yards in the 1933 Open Championship. At that time, as it is today, it was one of the most renowned par-three holes in golf and one of the most difficult. Its tee sits as high as any point on the course; a player can be required to hit anything from a pitching wedge to a 4-iron, depending on the strength and direction of the wind. The green is severely sloped from back to front. Its most daunting features are the two infamous bunkers that guard the right and left front of the green. The one on the right is called Strath Bunker. It is a pot bunker that can often force a player to play his next shot back toward the tee. Hill Bunker on the left side is the more treacherous of the two, large in size and ultra-deep.

It is very admirable that Bobby Jones would incorporate a great likeness to the 11th at St. Andrews, considering that it was at that hole in the 1921 Open Championship that Jones suffered his famous meltdown, previously described in chapter 4. He called it "the most inglorious failure of my golfing life." The 1921 British Open was Jones's first appearance at St. Andrews. His great respect and admiration for the Old Course did not develop in a rapid fashion. It would take winning a British Open there in 1927 before his endearment to the layout was forever fortified.

Whereas the Bobby Jones debacle at the 11th in the 1921 Open Championship is the most talked about due to his later accomplishments, Gene's debacle at the 11th in 1933 is more noteworthy for its impact on the outcome of the tournament. Gene was in the thick of the hunt as he stood on the 11th tee and gauged the wind that day in the second round. He was a little quick on his downswing and pulled his ball into Hill Bunker. He took out his sand wedge. It was no longer a prototype— Wilson had taken Gene's design and put it into full production, and golfers far and wide were scooping them up. On this day, Hill Bunker proved to be too formidable for Gene and his sand wedge. In his first attempt from the deep bunker, he took too much sand and barely moved the ball. His second attempt needed just an inch more altitude. It caught the lip and rolled back almost to its previous position.

In a fit of temper, Gene waved his sand wedge in a forceful way at the lip of the bunker. He then decided not to take any more chances and played his ball sideways out of the bunker. This shot placed his ball on the green, but some 60 feet from the cup. His first approach putt was a poor one. It came up six feet short. Fortunately for Gene, his next effort found the bottom of the cup.

Gene would later call his play of the 11th that day the most torturous experience he had ever gone through in golf, because although he had holed out, controversy as to what he had actually scored on the hole was about to erupt and continue for the next several hours. As he was departing the green, Gene gave his score of six to the official scorer. An official who was marshaling the crowd from some distance away from Hill Bunker heard Gene say his score was six. He came over and told Gene his score was not a six but a seven.

At that point, Gene recounted his strokes on the hole and still came up with six. He then checked with the official scorer, who was Nan Baird, a former Scottish Ladies Champion, and her response was that she had counted six strokes as well. Then the marshal counted out Gene's strokes and he came up with seven. As he had construed from his vantage point, Gene's violent waving of his club at the lip of the bunker after his second shot failed was a wild whiff of the ball.

Gene tried to explain to the marshal that he did not make a stroke at the ball but the marshal refused to buy it. Their confrontation ended with the marshal advising Gene he felt compelled to report the fact he disputed Gene's score on the hole to the Championship Committee.

Word spread throughout the course like a brush fire—as bad as recording a six was that Gene may have been guilty of understating his score.

To Gene's credit, despite his poor play at the 11th hole and the hubbub over his score, he was able to par in and post a score of even par, which still left him in the hunt for the championship. After signing his card, he left the course and returned to his hotel room without bothering to change out of his golf shoes. He sat down in a chair and lit a cigar. Gene and his cigar shared something in common—they both were doing a slow burn. This was the first time in his golf career that his integrity had been questioned, and he was devastated by it.

Gene had only been in his chair for a few minutes when he received word from the hotel's front desk that the Championship Committee had called and requested that he come to meet with them in the clubhouse as soon as possible.

Gene changed his shoes and donned a jacket. Once at the clubhouse of the R&A he was ushered into a large room where he found 12 somber gentlemen seated at a long conference table. The spokesman of the group coolly stated that Gene's presence had been requested because his score of six at the 11th hole had been disputed by the marshal. He said the Championship Committee would like to hear Gene's side of the story.

In his autobiography, Gene recalled his response. It was brief but on point: "You gentlemen awarded me the honor of having the Scottish

Ladies Champion as my scorer. She signed my card. Isn't that sufficient?"

After a few moments of consultation, the committee threw out the marshal's protest. But its effect was not over. Gene spent a restless night, upset that his honesty had been called into question.

By morning, Gene had resolved to try and place the whole incident behind him and give the final day's 36 holes his best shot. In the morning round, he shot even par and remained in the hunt. In the afternoon round, Gene rolled in a couple of birdies, while the other contenders were making bogeys. When he reached the par-five 14th tee, barring a disaster, the tournament was his.

Situated in the landing area of second shots on the 14th, just over 100 yards from the green, is another of the Old Course's signature bunkers. It is very wide and very deep and is appropriately named "Hell Bunker." It is this bunker that produced Jack Nicklaus's most embarrassing moment in a major championship. In the 1995 Open Championship, Jack's second shot strayed into Hell; it took four shots to extricate his ball from its clutches, and he made a 10.

For Gene, landing in Hell Bunker would play a huge part in denying him back-to-back Open Championships. At the 14th tee, his drive was solid. Wary of Hell Bunker, he aimed well left of it with his fairway wood second shot. His plan was good, but his execution wasn't. He caught the shot on the heel of the club and it drifted right—well right—and into Hell Bunker. Gene's first attempt from Hell missed clearing its high lip by a few inches and plugged into its face. It took one shot just to get his ball out of the face. Laying four and still in the bunker, Gene's next shot escaped Hell's clutches and reached the green, but it set some 35 feet from the pin. His putt for bogey missed. His putt for double bogey missed as well. His putt for triple bogey, which was still in knee-knocking range, dropped for an eight. Gene parred in and waited, as the other contenders were in groups behind him.

When the day was over, Americans Craig Wood and Denny Shute finished tied. Gene and two others were one stroke behind them. The combined total of six strokes he had expended in escaping the clutches of Hill and Hell bunkers had killed his chance at two Open Championships in a row. Shute defeated Wood in the play-off the next day by five strokes.

The PGA had announced the schedule for the 1933 Ryder Cup in mid-December of 1932. In early January 1933, the USGA and the R&A had set the dates for their Open championships in June and early July respectively. The schedule for the PGA Championship was still to be determined when the U.S. Ryder Cup team set sail for England in mid-June. The PGA Championship had typically taken place in late summer. It had also taken place once in October, once in November, and once in December.

While 10 of the PGA's top names were in St. Andrews wrapping up their first day of competition in the qualifying rounds for the British Open on July 3, 4,000 miles away in Chicago, the PGA announced it was going to hold the PGA Championship beginning August 8 at the Blue Mound Country Club outside of Milwaukee, Wisconsin, and that sectional qualifying would take place in three weeks.

A few days after the British Open concluded, the PGA received quite a shock. Walter Hagen, a five-time winner of the PGA Championship, would not be in Milwaukee to compete. Neither would the newly crowned British Open champion Denny Shute. In the run-up to the Open Championship, Hagen and Shute had signed contracts to stay in Great Britain for an additional three weeks and play in a series of exhibition matches.

Gene's participation was also in doubt. He and Joe Kirkwood had planned to resume their tour in the Aero car, with a schedule mapped out to conclude in mid-August with a match against U.S. Open winner Johnny Goodman in Omaha. Several other members of the Ryder Cup team were also considering bypassing the event.

Tommy Armour, who had been Gene's staunch ally in the Billy Burke controversy with the PGA, took harsh exception to the possibility of Gene and the others skipping the PGA Championship, as he believed they were killing the goose that laid the golden egg. Gene was not swayed by Tommy's analogy. In an interview with Alan Gould of the Associated Press that ran in the *Washington Post*, Gene laid the blame at the feet of the PGA hierarchy and their lackadaisical approach to scheduling the event. As to his allegiance to the PGA, Gene said, "Our loyalty to the PGA is one thing and our business of making a living out of golf another."

Hoping to give the area hit hard by the Depression a shot in the arm, the Milwaukee businessmen who had agreed to sponsor the PGA Championship were upset over the possible absence of golf's biggest names, and announced that they would withdraw their support unless every member of the Ryder Cup team participated.

To try and get a handle on the situation, the PGA announced that it would wave sectional qualifying for all members of the Ryder Cup team and automatically place them in the medal round at Blue Mound that would determine the 32 players who would take part in the match play competition for the championship.

Gene was playing an exhibition in Rochester, New York, with Joe Kirkwood when he received word about the PGA's concession on qualifying, and decided that he would change his plans and enter the event. The PGA cabled Hagen and Shute in England and pleaded with them to reconsider.

It was reported that Hagen and Shute had decided to discontinue their tour and would be setting sail for home at once. Their anticipated arrival date would give them just enough time to reach Milwaukee for the championship. Twenty-four hours later that report turned out to be inaccurate; Hagen and Shute were staying in Great Britain, where they had been drawing big crowds on their exhibition tour. This was unfortunate because Hagen was playing his best golf in years. He had finished fourth in the U.S. Open and had held the lead for two rounds at the British Open. On his tour with Shute, Hagen had set new course records at three different clubs on three successive days.

As it ended up, Gene was joined in the field by six of the remaining seven Ryder Cup members. This was enough star power for the sponsors to remain committed to the event.

The Blue Mound Country Club was built in 1926 and had three strong years before the Crash of 1929. Although it was now in receivership, it was in adequate shape to host the event. It was not long by any means at 6,200 yards, but its tricky greens made up for its shortcomings in distance.

Gene was one of the last players to arrive, getting to Blue Mound in the afternoon before the medal-play qualifying. The next day he made the field of 32 with relative ease, shooting two under for 36 holes. Once the match play began, Gene breezed through his first 36-hole match, taking down Vincent Elred eight-up with seven to play. His second match proved to be his toughest. It was a four-and-three win over Harry Cooper. In the quarter-finals, Gene defeated Ed Dudley, five and four. In the semifinals Gene went up against his good friend Johnny Farrell and polished him off five and four.

In the finals, Gene opposed Willie Goggin, the Cinderella story of the event. Goggins was the professional for a municipal course in San Francisco. In reaching the finals, he had knocked off three of the biggest names in the field: Leo Diegel, Paul Runyan, and Al Espinosa. Goggins played Gene strong in the morning 18 and was only one down. In the afternoon round, Gene's putter caught fire. He closed out Goggins at the 31st to take a five-up with four to go decision to claim his third PGA championship and the sixth major of his career.

Gene closed out 1933 on the exhibition circuit. In mid-December the PGA, recognizing the error of its ways in scheduling its showcase event, announced its tournament committee for the coming year. The eight chosen were all players. The chairman of the committee was Leo Diegel. The other seven members were Gene, Paul Runyan, Craig Wood, Al Espinosa, Horton Smith, Olin Dutra, and Johnny Farrell.

12

"HAS ANYBODY BEEN BOTHERING THE LAMBS?"

In the late 1960s and early 1970s, one of Gene's favorite golf tales he enjoyed sharing in interviews and on the banquet circuit was that one day while two golfers were playing a round, they observed two large planes flying overhead. One of them said to the other, "There goes Nicklaus and Palmer." A few moments later, they saw two small planes flying in the same direction, which prompted the other golfer to say, "And there go their caddies." To a large degree, a similar story could have been told about Gene, as he was one of the first golfers to embrace air travel and he did in a big way. In January 1934, Gene announced that he and Joe Kirkwood would be making an exhibition tour in Central and South America in the spring. On the trip, the two would travel some 10,000 miles by plane.

In any other year, Gene and Joe's tour would have gotten an abundance of play in the press. But this was far from a typical year when it came to golf. The week Gene and Joe would go wheels up on their South American excursion, there would be a golf event that would overshadow anything else taking place on the nation's sports scene. The fuse for this happening had been ignited in late October when the schedule was announced for the professional golfer's winter circuit. It featured 16 tournaments that crisscrossed the country. The first event would be in the Washington, DC, area in mid-November. From there it moved to Pinehurst No. 2 for the Mid-South Open. The third stop, in early December, would be in Miami at Gene's home club in the winter, the Miami-Biltmore, for the

Miami-Biltmore Open. After a two-week break, the tour would move to the West Coast for events in Southern California and San Francisco. The West Coast swing would end the first week of February at Agua Caliente. It would then work its way back to the Southeast and conclude with another stop at Pinehurst No. 2 for the North and South Open the last weekend in March.

What was causing all the hubbub about the schedule was its next-to-last stop. It was a new event to be held at Bobby Jones's Augusta National Golf Club: The Augusta National Invitational. Having an event on a course created by the greatest player the game had ever known would have been enough to generate loads of appeal, but something else was added to the announcement that moved the event into the "tremendous interest" category. Jones, who had retired from the game over three years earlier at the age of 30, was making a comeback of sorts. He was not only going to host the event; he was also going to make a one-time exception to his retirement and compete, as well.

From this point until the curtain dropped at the first Augusta National Invitational, the golf world—and that of a large percentage of sports fans in general—focused on Augusta and Bobby Jones. Early on, as article after article rolled off the presses, the tournament's official name often took a back seat. Although it would not be formally changed until 1939, the name "the Masters" began to circulate in its place.

Just a few weeks after the announcement, Jones was in Pinehurst to watch the pros play in the second event on the winter tour and to test some of the new Spalding clubs that now bore his name. While the pros were playing Pinehurst No. 2, Bobby was playing Pinehurst No. 1, often hitting multiple shots from the same location. The gallery following him far exceeded any that the pros had over at the tournament.

During his almost four-year absence from the competitive scene, no other player could develop the emotional ties to the fans that Jones had achieved. Often the biggest rush at the U.S. Opens since Jones retired was when he would be spotted in the gallery and then be engulfed by autograph seekers.

As the days ticked by toward the late March date of the first Masters, Jones played as much golf as possible. In late December, in a slight rain and a cold wind, he played in an exhibition at the opening of a municipal course in Atlanta named for him and shot a 67.

Shortly after the new year began, Jones made several trips from his Atlanta home down to Augusta to check on preparations for the tournament and to work on his game. To those who had seen him play, he displayed no ill effects from the switch. His swing was as smooth and flawless as ever. His foot and hip movements were as rhythmic as they had been in his glory days.

Jones was four years removed from the height of those glory days, his Grand Slam having taken place in 1930. Yet his accomplishments had not lost any of their luster, as evidenced by a poll conducted by the Associated Press six weeks before Augusta National's inaugural event. In the poll, the AP asked 50 of the nation's leading sportswriters to rate the top sports performer for the period 1923 through 1933.

Given that Babe Ruth had been the superstar of the nation's pastime during the period covered by the poll, leading the New York Yankees to five American League pennants, four World Series crowns, and had hit 448 of his 714 home runs during the poll's time frame, one would have thought he would have come out on top. But Ruth finished in the second spot behind Bobby Jones by a five-vote margin.

Some of the others in the poll's top 10 were boxing greats Jack Dempsey and Gene Tunney, football star Red Grange, and tennis great Bill Tilden. The next highest finish for a golfer in the field was in the 15th spot, and was known as the female Bobby Jones, Glenna Collett Vare. During the span covered by the poll, which was long before there was a professional golf tour for women, she won four of her six U.S. Amateur titles, including three years in a row from 1928 through 1930.

During one of his last rounds that winter at Augusta, Jones recorded five birdies and an eagle and finished the round with a 67. This added plenty of fuel to the fire for those who thought Jones would be a force to be reckoned with when his tournament began—and who could blame them? After all, Jones was the greatest player the game had ever known. He was still just 32 years old. Almost all of his fellow competitors would be playing the course for the first time, while Jones had assisted in the Augusta National's design, supervised its construction, and the 67 he had recently shot there was the lowest score to date on the course.

Although a generous portion of the press and the public were optimistic about Jones's chances in the first Masters, there were a number of others that were highly skeptical of his prospects. Gene was among them. A week before the first Masters, Gene was in Washington, DC, where he was hyping his South American tour. In an interview with a reporter from the *Washington Post* that ran in the *Post*'s weekly golf column, "Down the Fairway," Gene was asked about Jones's chances. He gave this terse reply: "Jones has been gone too long."

At about the same time, Horton Smith, who had recorded 15 tournament wins since turning professional six years earlier, was also interviewed on the subject of Jones. Smith was also of the opinion that Jones would not be a factor at the Augusta National Invitational, and gave a detailed answer as to why. He believed that many of the American golf professionals who had gone up against Jones in U.S. Opens were under a psychological grip that he was unbeatable. Smith felt that this would not be the case now. He believed that the pros now playing the circuit were of a much higher caliber and greater in number than what Jones had faced during his heyday. They would look on him as a great golfer, but not invincible. Smith recognized that Jones's swing mechanics appeared to be intact, despite the long lay-off. But he had deep doubts as to whether Jones would be able to reconnect with the mental aspects of the game with the same sharpness he had exhibited prior to his retirement.

The first day of the first Masters was played in brilliant sunshine. Oddsmakers had the two favorites as Bobby Jones and Paul Runyan. The latter had won 12 tournaments over the last 15 months. The two were paired and went off at 10:35 a.m. In that opening round, Jones was hitting tee and approach shots that would have been the dream of any golfer, but his short game was a nightmare, especially his putting, the part of the game where the mental aspect that Horton Smith commented on is so vital.

Attendance that first day was sparse by the standards of today's Masters, just several thousand, and practically all of them were following Jones. They oohed and aahed over his tee shots, cheered his approach shots, and let out tremendous moans when his putts failed to fall. On two of the par fives, Bobby had tapped in birdies after missing very makeable eagle putts, one from inside four feet.

For the first two years of Augusta National's existence, the current front side was the back nine and current back side was the front nine. The roars from the patrons that sweep across Augusta National during the Masters are fabled. Ironically, when he was perhaps having the worst putting day of his career, it was a putt from Bobby Jones that created the first ever of these booming roars. It came on Bobby's backside at the long par-three 13th (now the fourth hole). As he had been all day, he was in good form off the tee and dropped his tee shot onto the green some 15 feet from the hole. When it came time for his attempt at birdie, he demonstrated the same bad form he had all day. In golfing parlance, he killed it. As his ball streaked toward the hole, Jones was aghast. He was sure he would be looking at a putt coming back as long as he had had to begin with. Then something unexpected happened—it hit the hole dead-center. Actually, it was more like crashed into it. His ball hit the back of the hole with such force it almost popped out. When it did disappear, the gallery let loose with that inaugural Augusta National roar.

When the day was over, Bobby had tallied a four over par 76. His playing partner, Paul Runyan, was two strokes better with a 74. Horton Smith shared the lead with two others at two-under-par 70.

On day two, Bobby spent close to an hour on the practice green and was rolling in everything. As he finished his warm-up and headed for the first tee, he joked that he hoped he was not leaving his stroke on the practice green. He did all right until the back nine. Then he three-putted 14 and 15, and missed from 18 inches on 16. He finished the day with a 74 and stood eight strokes off the lead.

That evening, Bobby was yearning to have his old putter Calamity Jane back in his bag. But she was on a shelf at the Spalding factory in Chicopee, Massachusetts, where she had been used as a model for the putter that was part of the Bobby Jones line of clubs. The logistics available in 1934 did not provide him any chance of a rush shipment that would arrive in time, so he opted to try for what would be the next best option. He needed help from his mother. Well, not actually from her personally, but from her golf bag. He remembered that years earlier he had given his mother a Calamity Jane–styled putter. He put in a call to a friend in Atlanta and had him go out to the bag room at the East Lake Golf Club and retrieve the putter from his mother's bag and bring it to him.

With Calamity Jane's cousin in his bag, Bobby played the last 36 holes at even par. He finished ten strokes behind the winner, Horton Smith, who had edged out Craig Wood by a stroke.

While the curtain was coming down at the first Masters, Gene was wrapping up a round in San Juan, Puerto Rico, a stopover on his way to South America. At that locale's Berwind Country Club, he shot a 66, which was a course record.

Before departing for the next stop, Gene was asked about Jones's performance in Augusta. He said that he was far from surprised, and believed that it would take Jones at least a year of competition to regain his old form. And even then, he might not be able to compete with the new crop of players, who displayed no fear of the old-timers. In an exchange that was carried by the *New York Times* the following day, Gene was then asked whether he considered himself an old-timer. Gene, who had recently turned 32, shot back, "Not by a long shot. Before last year they thought I was washed up . . . I am going to take a long time washing up."

From Puerto Rico, Gene and Joe Kirkwood flew to British Guiana and then on to Brazil, Argentina, and Peru. At about the halfway point of the tour, Gene dropped a note to Dave Herman at the *Washington Post*. The letter began with "We are still alive." This affirmation was likely due to the perils he and Joe were encountering on their flights between cities and countries. These hops often took place in outmoded aircraft. Their pilots often had to navigate their way through or over mountain ranges. In some of these instances, Gene and Joe were required to don oxygen masks. Takeoffs and landings regularly occurred on unpaved and often muddy runways.

The perils of South American air travel in the 1930s aside, Gene and Kirkwood were well received at all of their stops and drew good crowds. They were unbeaten in all their matches except one. In Buenos Aires, Argentina, they fell in a match, two and one, to the Bobby Jones of Argentina, José Jurado, and another top Argentine pro, Marcos Churio.

Gene and Joe arrived back in the States in mid-May, some four weeks ahead of the U.S. Open, which was going to take place at the Merion Cricket Club outside of Philadelphia. On the eve of the Open, there was plenty of coverage in the press about who stood the best chance. Gene was telling anyone that would listen that it would be either him, Walter Hagen, or Tommy Armour. Numerous others were just as sure the winner would come out of a new guard trio: Paul Runyan, Craig Wood, or Ky Laffoon. Runyan had been the winningest professional over the last two years. Wood had finished third in the 1933 U.S. Open, second in the 1933 British Open, and had recently finished second in the inaugural Masters at Augusta. Laffoon had won the Phoenix Pro-Am and the Atlanta Open and had been in the top five at a number of events on the winter tour.

The Merion Cricket Club, now known as the Merion Golf Club, has been home to a number of the game's most memorable moments. In 1916, Merion hosted a men's USGA event for the first time, the U.S. Amateur, and Bobby Jones made his debut in that event at the age of 14. Eight years later, Merion hosted its second U.S. Amateur and Bobby Jones was the winner. In 1930, Merion played host to the U.S. Amateur for a third time and it was again won by Bobby Jones. It was the victory that completed his historic Grand Slam. The 1934 U.S. Open was the first of five Opens that Merion has hosted. Its second Open in 1950 produced the game of golf's most iconic photo: Ben Hogan in his follow-through with a 3-iron shot that would produce a par at the 72nd hole and place him in an 18-hole play-off that he won the following day.

Gene loved the Merion course. After a practice round he called it "a course second to none." Merion wasn't long, but it required control and accuracy from the tee and on approach shots.

The bookmakers settled on Gene and Paul Runyan as their top choices to win at Merion. The USGA made them the marquee pairing for the first two rounds. After those two rounds, Paul was well back in the pack but Gene was in the mix near the top of the leaderboard, three strokes off the pace. At the end of round three, he was three shots ahead.

As Gene stepped onto the 11th tee in the final round, he appeared to be well on the road to his third U.S. Open title. He had maintained his three-shot lead. In second place was Olin Dutra, who was several groups behind Gene in the final pairing of the day.

The par-four 11th hole had been a turning point for Gene in the second round. He had almost hooked his tee shot into a creek, but missed it with just a few feet to spare. He hit his second shot high over a tree that stood between him and the green. In his wrap-up of the event, Grantland Rice dubbed it "the shot of the tournament." It landed safely on the green 30 feet from the hole. Gene then drained the putt, given his erratic drive a very improbable birdie.

In the third round, Gene had decided to play it safe off the tee at the 11th. He left his driver in the bag and used a 2-iron off the tee. His drive found the middle of the fairway and he made par. When Gene arrived at the 11th in the final round, he again went with the 2-iron strategy. This time it failed—he hit a big roping hook that splashed into the creek. After his drop, he was almost in the same position as he had been in the second round. But this time his approach didn't quite make it over the tree. It nipped some branches and fell short of the green. Gene's next shot was long and over the green. He chipped to four feet but missed the putt for a triple bogey seven.

Gene parred the next six holes. At the 18th, he missed a four-footer for par. A half-hour later, Olin Dutra made a tap of a few inches at the 18th hole for a one-stroke victory over Gene.

A little more than two weeks later, Gene was on the south coast of England at Sandwich for the British Open. This time it was being played at the Royal St. George's course adjacent to the Prince's course. During the U.S. Open, in a conversation with Paul Gallico, Gene had said he was "tired of golf." A week on the ocean appeared to have been just what he needed to revive his game. During practice rounds, he had the galleries buzzing with his shot making. The oddsmakers were impressed as well, and made him the favorite. It would have been hard not to—in the last two British Opens he had won one and finished one stroke out of a play-off in the other. And in his two recent U.S. Opens he had a first and a second.

Even with his recent impressive record in golf's two biggest events, he was in the same boat as the other 312 entries. He had to qualify. Gene played well on the first day of qualifying and appeared to be in position to make the field with ease, but things got a little testy on day two. He was caught in a rainstorm on his back nine and struggled mightily for six holes. His score ballooned, and there were some anxious moments until all the scores were posted. When they were, he was in the field by two strokes.

Purely based on numbers, the domination of the British Open by Americans was thought to be at risk, as participation from the States was very light. There were just four Americans in the field: Gene; Denny Shute, the event's defending champion; Joe Kirkwood; and Macdonald Smith. Gene had fared quite well in his two previous trips to Sandwich for British Opens. In 1928, he had finished second to Hagen at Royal St. George's and in 1932 had won at Prince's. On both of those occasions the late Skip Daniels was on his bag. Gene would sorely miss Skip.

Claiming Gene's bag was too heavy, his new caddy abruptly quit at the first tee of the first round. The replacement who scurried out was from deep down the caddie master's depth chart. Once Gene was finally under-way, a storm blew in and he was pelted with hailstones as he went down the first fairway. Despite the adversity, his approach on this par four left him a very makeable birdie opportunity. He failed to convert his birdie attempt and then missed his par putt.

It was a horrid beginning for what would be a very long day. There would be two more three-putts and several other makeable birdie putts missed. He finished the day with a 75 and was well back in the pack. He would remain back in the pack for the rest of the Open Championship. He finished 19 strokes behind the winner, Englishman Henry Cotton. Joe Kirkwood and Horton Smith were the low Americans, finishing in a three-way tie for fourth, nine strokes behind Cotton.

Before leaving the States for the British Open, Gene sent cold chills down the spines of PGA officials when he said there was a good chance he would not defend his PGA title; instead, he and Joe Kirkwood would do an extended exhibition tour of Europe. Fortunately for the PGA, their biggest drawing card would be in the field, as Gene and Joe's plans for a European tour fell through.

The PGA Championship was being played at the Park Country Club in Williamsville, New York, a suburb northeast of Buffalo. The ocean liner that brought Gene back from Great Britain docked in New York City three days before the first round was to begin. He did not have to qualify, as the PGA had adopted the practice of giving the defending champion an exemption into the field.

In his first match, Gene faced off against Herman Barron. He struggled for the first 27 holes and then rallied from two down to win to take a two-and-one victory.

A few days after his PGA victory the year before, Gene told a Chicago reporter that it had been a letter from Mary that he received just before the matches began that had spurred him to victory. Although Mary was present in spirit, she was where Gene believed a wife needed to be when her husband was competing in a major championship—at home. Gene had developed this attitude over the years, believing that having one's spouse at a big event was too much of a distraction. After his win at Milwaukee, he espoused his views on the matter in a magazine interview that was later excerpted in newspapers nationwide:

> The hand that rocks the cradle is rocking a lot of golf's finest professionals into bankruptcy and mediocrity. The saddest thing in golf isn't a muffed two-foot putt that loses a big championship, it's those zealous, jealous, gossiping wives of our playing professionals, who haunt their husbands; and watch them fire every shot in a money tournament

or an open championship. It's time the shackled pros, rose in a body and told them to stay home . . . [and] sew buttons on the old man's shirts. These women are the curse of golf to-day.

Gene's second round match against Al Watrous was all square after the first 18 holes, but then Watrous romped over him in the afternoon 18 to take the match four and three. One could easily make the case that Gene's play in that match could have been affected by a distraction of a different nature—a four-legged variety.

In 1933, Gene had begun to prepare for the day he would have to make a living outside of golf, a day it turned out would never come. He acquired a farm, and as a result acquired a nickname from his contemporaries, "the Squire." The farm was a 125-acre spread in Brookfield, Connecticut. He sold it 10 years later in 1944 and shortly thereafter purchased another farm. This one was 300 acres in Germantown, New York, and he would own it until the late 1960s.

After his match the day before, an admirer of Gene's had presented him with two lambs for his farm. Gene doted over the two lambs. He took the lambs over to an area beside the first-aid tent and tethered them to a tree. To make sure they were safeguarded that evening, he spent the night in the first-aid tent.

When Gene exited the green of the 15th hole after his match concluded, a reporter asked about the match. He said, "Al was just too good." Then he asked the reporter, "Has anybody been bothering the lambs?"

After the PGA, Gene spent the next several weeks at his Connecticut farm. In mid-August he and Joe Kirkwood departed for a far western swing of exhibitions that would take them into Canada and end in Vancouver in the middle of September. From there, they would sail for Australia by way of Hawaii. In addition to playing exhibitions in Australia, they would also be playing in several big events. Despite the big-event portion of the schedule, Mary Sarazen did accompany her husband on the trip.

When they arrived in Australia they faced an exhaustive pace. Their itinerary consisted of over 50 exhibitions in less than two months, requiring them to travel up and down the east coast of Australia.

Three weeks into their stay, Gene and Joe took part in the Australian Open played at the Royal Sydney Golf Club. After two rounds, Gene stood six strokes off the pace. In round three, he broke the course record of 69 and moved into the thick of the battle for the title. He struggled on the front nine of his final round and early on the back nine. He caught fire at the 13th hole with a birdie and proceeded to birdie 14, 15, and 16. It turned out that he needed one more birdie and a par to tie for first, but his putting stroke let him down. He three-putted the 17th and the 18th holes and finished in second, three strokes behind Australian professional Billy Bolger.

Joe Kirkwood finished two spots behind Gene in fourth place. Over the course of the event, Joe had received an abundance of press coverage on two fronts—his play in the tournament, and a dispute he was having with the Victoria Golf Association.

In three weeks, the Association would be the host of the next two big golf happenings on the Australian golf calendar, the Centenary Open and a match-play event involving teams from Australia, the United States, and Great Britain. Eight more prominent American professionals, their travel underwritten by the PGA, would be arriving to take part in these two events; both were to be played at the Metropolitan Golf Club in Melbourne.

In the intervening three weeks, Gene and Joe had several exhibitions scheduled at Melbourne-area clubs that belonged to the Victoria Golf Association. Fearing that these exhibitions would diminish interest in their upcoming events, the Association issued an edict barring those clubs from hosting Gene and Joe until after their events.

This infuriated Joe. He and Gene would not be available for the second event. They would be moving on to New Zealand, but had planned to play in the first event, the Melbourne Centenary Open. Joe initiated a war of words with the Association, indicating that he and Gene were considering withdrawing from the Centenary Open events unless their edict was rescinded. The Association refused to yield and called Joe's bluff. He folded.

In the Centenary Open, Gene finished in third place. The winner was Jimmy Thomson from Los Angeles, one of the eight from the contingent of professionals sent over by the PGA. In the second tournament, a match-play event, the Americans dominated. The semifinals were an all-American affair. Leo Diegel claimed the title, downing Denny Shute two and one.

Gene enjoyed the sights and golf in New Zealand but he cut his stay short, returning to the States several weeks earlier than expected after he and Joe had a disagreement over one of the financial aspects of their tour.

13

JONES'S FINAL FLURRY

The Sarazens greeted 1935 on the Pacific. Their ship docked in San Francisco on January 4. From San Francisco, they drove over to Sacramento for the Sacramento Open and then down to Los Angeles for the LA Open. Gene's performance in both events was flat.

Also in the Los Angeles area during the LA Open was Grantland Rice. He was about halfway through his 35-year run as the country's preeminent sportswriter. Rice was following a winter schedule that had become the norm for him in recent years—he would spend January and February in the Los Angeles area. What brought him to Southern California was his daughter and only child, Florence. She was pursuing a career in Hollywood as an actress. Rice played a considerable amount of golf during these visits. He joined the Lakeview Country Club, which was the home course of some of Hollywood's biggest names.

In early March, Rice would go to Florida for two purposes: to play in the annual Artists and Writers Golf Association tournament in Palm Beach, and to cover Major League Baseball's spring training. The golf tournament started in the early 1920s and continued until the start of World War II. It was quite an affair for about three dozen very zealous golfers whose ranks included cartoonist Rube Goldberg and columnist, short story writer, and playwright Ring Lardner. Rice was the driving force behind the golf tournament and, more times than not, its defending champion. When the baseball teams were close to breaking camp, Rice would head back to his base in New York City. On the way back, his itinerary now included a lengthy stopover in Augusta.

A few days before the LA Open, Gene had sat down for an interview with Rice. When the piece ran the next day, it covered Gene's extensive travel during 1934. Gene heaped praise on Australia and New Zealand, complimenting their climates, golf courses, and citizens.

During this interview, Rice brought up Gene's darkest moment in golf during 1934, his debacle at Merion's 11th hole during the U.S. Open. Gene gave Rice a frank assessment, one that he had not previously shared with the press. His undoing at the 11th hole that day had been his pride and conscience.

When it came time to take a drop after his ball had flown into the creek, Gene chose to ignore one option that was available to him. He could have gone as far back from the spot where his ball entered the creek, as long as he kept the spot where his ball had entered it between where he took his drop and the hole. If he had taken this option, he could have gone back far enough to easily clear the tree that was in his line of flight. The basis for waiving this option could be traced back to that brouhaha with Hagen in the finals of the 1923 PGA, detailed in chapter 5. Although the drop Gene took in that instance was executed after he consulted with an official, after Hagen unsuccessfully challenged it, Gene sensed a mood in the gallery that he was trying to get away with something.

At Merion, Gene had wanted to go back a safe distance for the drop but was afraid he would be criticized by "some people." So he dropped his ball just a few feet from the hazard. His shot from that location nipped the tree and fell well short of the green, and a possible one-putt par or a likely bogey snowballed into a triple bogey seven.

Gene finished in a tie for fourth in the LA Open. The next week in the Sacramento Open he claimed the 10th spot. He was not a factor in the next two events, the San Francisco Match Play Open and the Oakmont Open in Glendale.

From Glendale, the tour headed across the border into Mexico for the Agua Caliente Open. The high-paying event was adding a new feature— pari-mutuel betting. Those in attendance were going to be allowed to pick the player who would shoot the lowest round each day for $2. No wagers were to be taken for the overall winner. Ninety percent of the pot would go to the purchasers. The remaining 10 percent would go into a pool that would be shared with the players who finished that day in the top three spots.

Gene was not going to the Agua Caliente; he was headed back to Connecticut to the pigs, cows, and lambs on his farm because he wanted no part of pari-mutuel betting, and he let anyone that would listen know about his displeasure. He believed pari-mutuel betting was fine for horse racing, but wrong for golf. In an interview with an Associated Press reporter that was carried in the *Los Angeles Times*, Gene opined:

> Golf is a game and it must continue to be a game for sportsmen to play and watch. You know and I know that nobody playing in the tournament would make a single move that was not absolutely on the up and up, but there are always people that will want to throw some dirt. No, sir, it's not for me.

While he was on his soapbox about pari-mutuel betting, Gene, in the same interview, also let loose about another issue: the spreading out of purses on tour. Citing the payout at the Oakmont in Glendale, he said,

> Macdonald Smith shot a great score in winning the Oakmont in California. . . . Out of the $6,500 purse, he received a mere $600. Thirty or forty other players split the rest. . . . Spreading the purse over a wide field has taken all the thrill out of winning these days. It is like playing for sandwich money now.

Gene had only been back at his farm for a few days when the press came knocking at his door seeking his comments on what Joe Kirkwood was saying about how he and Gene were treated during their tour of Australia. Joe was still making the rounds in the Far Pacific. In the Australian press, there were multiple reports that Joe was saying that Gene would likely never return because of the way he and Joe had been treated during their tour. In these accounts, Joe described their treatment "as being given the cold shoulder." Kirkwood's comments were picked up by wire services in the United States. This led to Gene being contacted for his reaction. Gene stated that Joe's comments were blatantly not true, and issued a very lengthy statement on the matter. In it he said he had never in fact "enjoyed such hospitality" and he was very much looking forward to a return trip in two years. Gene revealed that friction had developed between himself and Joe over the flap involving the Victoria Golf Association's barring of several of their scheduled exhibitions because, it turned out, Joe had known about the Association's stance on the matter before the two had even set sail for Australia.

Gene also revealed the reason for the disagreement in New Zealand that ended the duo's tour several weeks earlier than scheduled. He and Joe had clashed on what they should charge for admission to their exhibition matches. Joe's suggested price was twice as much as Gene wanted to charge. The two could not come to terms on the matter, and Gene told Joe "he would have to go it alone," and booked passage home.

After a few weeks in Connecticut, Gene headed to Florida to play in an international four-ball event in Miami and a match-play event in St. Augustine that teamed a professional with a top amateur. His play in both of these events was lackluster. From St. Augustine, Gene headed up the coast to Charleston, South Carolina, to join the winter tour at the Charleston Open. His performance there was also lackluster. He finished 15 strokes behind the winner, Henry Picard.

After the Charleston Open, the winter tour had a jam-packed conclusion. The event in Charleston wrapped up on a Saturday. The following Wednesday the tour was in Pinehurst for the North-South Open, which was, prior to the advent of the Masters, the winter tour's flagship event. This was the 33rd edition of this tournament. It started with single rounds on Wednesday and Thursday and a 36-hole final day on Friday. From Pinehurst, the pros would travel the 340-plus miles to Atlanta to tee it up the next day in Atlanta in the 54-hole Metropolitan Open. Its schedule called for 18 holes on Saturday and 36 holes on Sunday. From there most of the participants would head for Augusta for the Masters, which would kick off on Thursday.

Gene took a pass on the Pinehurst and the Atlanta tournaments and headed straight for Augusta. Since most of the field had played in the Masters the year before, he needed as much practice time there as he could get in to familiarize himself with the Augusta National layout. Gene was no stranger to Augusta. One of his first appearances on the winter circuit in 1920 was in an event at the Augusta Country Club, which was located adjacent to the property that would in 13 years become the Augusta National Golf Club. Gene earned his first professional winnings in the event—$75.

When Gene passed through the gates of Augusta National and headed down Magnolia Lane for the first time to the stately clubhouse, he was beginning an annual pilgrimage that would be replicated, with just a few exceptions, for the next 60-plus years.

Soon after his arrival on the grounds, Gene headed to the Augusta National Pro Shop to seek the assistance of his former Ryder Cup teammate Ed Dudley, the club's head professional. Gene wasn't seeking help with his swing. He needed Dudley's recommendation on equipment. The putter that Gene had used to win his last three major titles had disappeared from his bag. Dudley persuaded Gene to try a new model he had just received for his shop. It was a center-shafted model in the style of the old Schenectady.

Dudley's recommendation turned out to be pure gold. Gene's confidence on the demanding greens of Augusta increased with each round of practice. His confidence on the green began to work its way into the other facets of his game, and he turned in some very strong scores. His most impressive number was a 67.

While Gene got in an abundance of practice at Augusta National, a portion of the field did not. Bobby Jones had sent out 138 invitations to professionals and amateurs. Sixty-six accepted, but a large portion of that number did not get in a practice round until Tuesday of tournament week. A torrential rainstorm had pushed the final round of the tournament in Atlanta back a day, delaying the arrival in Augusta of almost half the field by a day.

Grantland Rice was also an early arrival in Augusta. He joined Gene for two of his practice rounds. In a column before the tournament, Rice touted Gene's play and picked him as one of his favorites. Rice was also picking his old friend Bobby Jones, despite his performance in 1934, among his favorites. He predicted that when the tournament reached its final round, Jones would be in the thick of it. Tommy Armour was also picking Jones to be a factor.

On Tuesday of tournament week, Jones was listed by the oddsmakers at eight to one, but the following day there was a big shift and Gene became the favorite at six to one. One of the features of most golf tournaments of this period was called a Calcutta. It was an auction of the players in the field, generally held on the eve of the tournament. The funds collected were placed in a pool, with the purchaser of the winner receiving a very generous portion of the proceeds.

Until the conducting of Calcuttas was discouraged by the USGA in the late 1940s, the largest Masters' Calcutta was conducted in a ballroom at the Bon Air Hotel on the eve of the tournament. In the Calcutta for the second Masters, as it had been for the first, the player who had brought the most at auction was Bobby Jones. He went for $625. Gene was next, bringing a price of $500. Rounding out the top five were Horton Smith, the winner of the 1934 Masters; Paul Runyan; and Ed Dudley, the host pro. Each of them went for $400.

For some reason, the bidders at the Bon Air Calcutta did not get too worked up over the hottest player in golf, Henry Picard. He was sold for just $300. Picard had won the Agua Caliente on the tour's West Coast swing and had won two of the three events before the Masters, the Charleston Open and the rain-delayed event in Atlanta that had a whopping payout to the winner of $400. At the North-South Open in Pinehurst, Picard took third place.

Day one of the second Masters got underway in a gray misty chill. At its peak, attendance for the day hovered at 1,000. The Bobby Jones comeback story teetered at the start—he bogeyed the first hole. He got back to even par on the very next hole with a birdie. Several other birdie opportunities went by the wayside on the front nine, and he posted an even par 36. On the back side, he had a birdie at 12 and three bogeys. One of those bogeys came at the easiest hole on the course, the par-five 13th. His score for the round was 74.

The leader of the first round was Henry Picard with a 67. His only bogey of the day came at the 18th, when he bunkered his approach and could not get up and down. Sarazen, Ray Mangrum, and Willie Goggin, who had an ace at the par-three 16th hole, were tied for second, one stroke back. Gene could have easily been the leader but his putting, which had been so strong in his practice rounds with his new putter, was spotty and he missed four putts from the three- to six-feet range.

Before the start of the tournament, Tommy Armour was pressed by reporters to explain why he had picked Bobby Jones as one of the favorites to win the Masters. His response, which was carried in the *Washington Post*, was "Because he is the type that can get hot on a moment's notice and burn up any course." For an hour during the second round, just as the morning's gray clouds gave way to brilliant sunshine, Bobby Jones caught fire.

At the first tee, almost all of the gallery had assembled and had flocked along with Jones. The first three holes were routine pars. At the par-three fourth, where par is always in doubt, he rattled in a knee-knocker for his three. At the par-four fifth, he chipped in for birdie. He parred the par-three sixth. Jones then made a big breaking putt at the par-four seventh for another birdie.

At the par-five eighth, the atmosphere became electric when Jones scorched a tee shot. He was well in range to reach the green in two. He took out a fairway wood and launched a shot that was tracking for the flag all the way. When his ball came to rest, it was just eight feet from the cup.

An eagle at the eighth would have given Jones his fifth three in a row. The gallery held its collective breath as Jones lined up his putt, waiting to let out a roar. Instead of a roar, they groaned. Jones's eagle putt did not drop and he had to settle for a tap-in birdie.

Jones made a no-stress par at nine and moved to the back nine with a gallery that was sure they were witnessing the return to the throne of the former king of golf. And who could blame them? In the first round, the lowest score that had been recorded by the field on the front nine was a 33. It was turned in by Picard, the first-round leader.

Those in the gallery had indeed witnessed something special, but it was not what any one of them would have wanted. It was last time Bobby Jones would display the type of play that had made him the greatest player the game had ever seen.

Jones started his back nine with another no-stress par, and then headed for the tee of the 11th hole, a par four. His drive from the 11th tee struck a tree branch late in its flight and ricocheted into the woods. Jones had to punch out and made a bogey. On the devilish par-three 12th, Jones dropped his tee shot in very makeable birdie range. He stroked a solid putt, but it rimmed out and he settled for par.

From the par-five 13th tee, Bobby's tee shot came up short for an attempt to get home in two. He laid up and then hit what looked like a perfect pitch, but it skipped 12 feet past the hole. His birdie putt slipped by the hole. He missed his par putt coming back and took a bogey six. Bobby then three-putted the 14th hole for another bogey, and for all practical purposes the book was closed on those pulling for a Bobby Jones comeback.

Gene had a front-row seat for the rise and fall of Bobby Jones in the second round—he was paired with him. Gene shot a one-under-par 71. His round could have been much better but, like Jones, he struggled around the greens and on them. His saving grace was the par fives. As he did in the first round, he birdied three of the four.

Other than Picard, only one other player broke 70 in the second round, Walter Hagen. His score of 69 was a bit of a surprise to almost everyone and a huge surprise to Paul Gallico, who was covering the Masters for the *Chicago Tribune.* Gallico had bumped into Hagen at an Augusta gambling hall at 2 a.m. Hagen's face was rose-colored. He had a stack of roulette chips in one hand and tall glass of Scotch in the other. News of Hagen's activities the night before had circulated among the press during the course of the day, and after his round Walter was quizzed about what time he had gone to bed. Walter stated that he had slipped into bed at 6 a.m. for a quick snooze before rising around nine. He had a glass of orange juice for breakfast and headed off for his 11 a.m. tee time.

Hagen was now 43 and prior to the 1935 winter circuit, most thought his age and lifestyle had caught up with him, as his tournament play had experienced a huge drop. Walter was also dealing with the after-effects of a tragedy that occurred the previous July during the St. Paul Open in Minnesota. On the evening after the first round, he was driving to where he was to overnight when a six-year-old boy darted out of the darkness and Walter's vehicle struck and killed him. But six weeks before the Masters Walter, who had not won a tournament in three years, won the Gasprilla Open in Tampa by one stroke with closing birdies at the 71st and 72nd holes.

Often an unfortunate circumstance—a bad bounce, a click of a camera, a putt that does a 180 and spins out of the hole—can be the trigger that sends a player's game into a downward spiral. Henry Picard experienced one of those circumstances on the third hole of his third round. For Picard, it was the suspected lack of care of a fellow competitor that took place—not on the course, but in the locker room—that would knock him off his game.

Picard had started his third round with two routine pars. One the par-four third hole, his approach shot found a greenside bunker. When Picard reached the edge of the trap, he asked his caddie for his sand wedge. The caddie could not find it. Picard did his own frantic search of the bag and he came up empty handed as well. A friend of Picard's in the gallery was dispatched to the locker room to search for the missing club. Meanwhile, Picard was forced to improvise his exit from the bunker with another club. His first effort did not escape the trap. His second attempt checked up just two feet from the cup. After all that had transpired, escaping with a bogey would have been considered a decent outcome. But it was not to be. Picard missed the two-footer and recorded a double-bogey. He then bogeyed the next two holes.

Picard's friend found the missing sand wedge and rushed back out to him. The friend had found it resting against a locker. It was surmised that a fellow competitor had removed it from Picard's bag to take a look at it and had failed to place it back in his bag.

Picard ended the day with a 76, which dropped him into third place, two strokes behind the new leader, Craig Wood, who had the sole round in the 60s for the day, a 68. Olin Dutra had second place, one stroke back. Sarazen had a one-over 73 and dropped back to fourth place, three behind Wood. Hagen stayed among the leaders with an even par 72, which left him in fifth.

Craig Wood was six feet tall and muscular with blonde hair. He was called "Golden Boy," but he was far from a boy. Wood, Sarazen, and Bobby Jones were all 33 years of age. Wood was the oldest by three months over Gene and four months over Jones.

Gene and Walter Hagen's formative years in golf had started in their early teens. Bobby Jones had played in his first U.S. Amateur at the age of 14. Henry Picard had started caddying in Massachusetts in his early teens and had taken his first assistant pro job in Charleston, South Carolina, at the age of 17. Craig Wood had started caddying at the age of seven, and by the time he was 12 he was shooting in the low 80s. At age 13, Wood gave up golf and his focus turned to his schooling, hockey, and baseball; Wood played both of those sports while in college at Clarkson Tech in Potsdam, New York. He dropped out of Clarkson after two years. A year or so later, Wood, now 20, was working as a bookkeeper in Kentucky. His job gave him some free time in the late afternoon, and he decided to venture back onto the golf course.

Wood had very solid fundamentals when he had given up the game. As a result, it took only a short time to get to where he was before he had taken leave of golf. He improved steadily from that point and in less than a year he landed an assistant pro's position.

Wood's first win came at the Kentucky Open in 1925. Over the next seven years, he averaged a couple of wins a year, but none of these victories were in top-drawer events.

In 1933, he joined the top tier of the game. He won the LA Open, finished second in the Agua Caliente, third in the U.S. Open, and second in the British Open, losing in a play-off at St. Andrews.

Wood was one of the game's longest hitters. He earned one of his biggest checks that year with his driver—not on the golf course, but in a football stadium, Chicago's Soldier Field. The World's Fair was in Chicago and a few days before the U.S. Open that was being held just outside of Chicago, the *Chicago American* newspaper put on a golf exhibition as part of the World's Fair at Soldier Field, which at that time was configured in the shape of a U. Players competed in a long-drive contest, and Wood won the event, taking home a check for $1,100.

At the British Open at St. Andrews, Wood created quite a buzz when he uncorked a drive, aided by a howling wind at his back and in very dry and hard conditions, that traveled over 400 yards on the Old Course's par-five fifth hole.

In 1934, Wood took second in the inaugural Masters. At the U.S. Open at Merion, like Gene, he had a disaster. Among the leaders late in the second round, Wood played the wrong ball from the rough and was disqualified.

At the PGA Championship several months later, Wood made it to the finals. His opponent produced quite a contrast—Wood the muscular Adonis against 125-pound, five-foot-seven Paul Runyan. Wood was a prolific smoker and played many of his shots during a round with a cigarette pressed in his lips. Runyan believed one of the keys to a good golf shot was having the right fit in underwear, and had his briefs tailor made. Runyan was a dancer of some renown, and liked to hum rumba and tango tunes as he walked down the fairway or when he was lining up putts. When Runyan sank a long putt, he would rumba to the hole to retrieve his ball.

Runyan had finished in a tie for third place at Augusta in 1934, one stroke behind Wood and two strokes behind Horton Smith, the winner. Smith's play off the tee had been a key component of his victory. He was using a driver Runyan had loaned him a few days before the start of the tournament.

The Runyan versus Wood PGA Championship final, won by Runyan in a play-off, had an ironic twist. It was Wood who had helped Runyan in a big way on his path to golfing success a half-dozen years earlier, by bringing him from his native Arkansas to New Jersey to be his assistant pro at the Forest Hill Field Club in Bloomfield, New Jersey.

14

THE SHOT

Late Sunday morning, April 7, 1935, at Augusta National did not seem like the day on which Gene Sarazen or anybody else would achieve golf immortality. It was cold and dreary. The course was soggy from off-and-on rain through the night.

Craig Wood, the leader at five under par, was being given the nod to be on top at the end of the day. If Wood faltered, the victor was expected to come from among those who occupied the next four spots on the leaderboard: Olin Dutra, one behind; Henry Picard, two behind; Gene, three behind; and Walter Hagen, four back.

Gene and Walter were paired and would be one of the last groups to tee off. The other three contenders went off well ahead of them. Since their match in the Unofficial World Championship, their relationship could be described from Gene's angle as rocking back and forth between amicable and surly. From Hagen's side, as it was with almost everyone, their association would fall in the area of 90 percent favorable, 10 percent contentious.

Walter was dressed in a resplendent blue sweater and matching knickers, and was up to his old tricks. His lingering on the putting green up to the last moment before their tee time irked Gene. He yelled out for somebody to "Bring Grandpa on."

Gene was anxious to get going, as things were unfolding on the course that brightened the outlook in both his and Walter's favor. At the third hole, where the day before Henry Picard had stumbled with a double bogey after a runaway performance in the first two rounds, Olin Dutra had stumbled in this final round. He duffed three shots in a row and was fortunate to make a double bogey. Olin had started with a bogey at the first and, after his debacle at three, he had bogeyed four as well. Craig Wood was two over in his round through five and Henry Picard was three over to that point.

For the first eight holes, Gene was the model of consistency with eight consecutive pars. On the other hand, the resurgent Walter had disappeared, and the stale Walter had returned. He was four over. Craig Wood had made the turn in three over 39 and was one over through 12 on the back, placing Gene and himself in a tie for the lead at that point.

The tie didn't last for long. Gene hit an errant drive and took a bogey at the ninth, while Craig made birdie at the par-five 13th to take a two-stroke lead. Gene bogeyed the 10th to drop three behind. Craig added another stroke to his lead at 14 when he picked up another birdie, but gave it back with a bogey at the par-three 16th. Craig parred the 17th. Gene's hopes were buoyed when he birdied the 13th to cut the margin to two. But they were dashed before he could get to the 14th tee when a roar went up from the 18th green. He suspected Craig had birdied the final hole.

At the 14th, Gene hit a dreadful tee shot, a duck hook that left him with a very long approach shot from the rough. As he was walking to his drive, Gene received confirmation that Craig Wood had birdied the 18th and now had a very comfortable looking three-stroke lead. Gene's approach shot made it to the green, but that was about all that could be said for it.

Up at the 18th green, Craig Wood was making his way toward the clubhouse after dropping a curling 12-foot birdie putt. The overall mood among those gathered at the 18th was that his closing birdie had put the tournament on ice. Wood was being slapped on the back by well-wishers, stopping for autographs and posing for photographers. Paul Gallico was standing atop the photographer's tower that overlooked the 18th green. During the course of his years covering golf, he had seen this scene play out a number of times. But on this occasion, it gave him an uneasy feeling.

On a course of demanding greens, the 14th is considered among the most daunting. It is huge in size and diabolical in the treacherous undulations it features. Gene's approach rested 100 feet from the cup. On this green, it was set in what was the epitome of three-putt territory. Gene's first putt travel 94 feet. This left him the embodiment of a knee-knocker. It dropped, keeping the distance between Gene and Craig at three strokes.

While Gene and Walter had been completing play of the 14th, Craig had made his way into the clubhouse and amidst a swarm of press had been reunited with his wife, Jacqueline. She was a lovely and charming petite woman in her early 30s with dark hair and dark eyes. Jacqueline had not followed her husband on the course. She opted to stay in the clubhouse with a number of other players' wives and pass the time in conversation. She kept one ear, however, dedicated to picking up any information that was swirling around about the happenings out on the course.

A year ago to the day, Jacqueline and Craig had been the center of attention at a much smaller and quieter affair, their wedding. The first Masters had been played in late March in 1934. After a heartbreaking second-place finish, Craig had traveled back to New York City to prepare for their nuptials. They were married in Jacqueline's apartment with just their immediate families and a few friends present.

Standing there, aglow with pride and happiness in the clubhouse, the Woods made quite the handsome couple. It was akin to a Hollywood ending, the player that had come so close the year before taking the big prize on his first wedding anniversary. Swept up in the moment, the couple submitted to a request to pose for a photograph with the winner's check.

By this time Gene and Walter were preparing to tee off at the par-five 15th. Gene was breathing an intense sigh of relief after draining his six-footer at 14 to save his par. If he had bogeyed, four back with four to go wasn't an insurmountable deficit, but it was close. Three back with four to go gave him a shot, albeit a long shot.

Bobby Jones was of the opinion that there was no duller hole in golf than a par-five on which a player had to hit three shots to reach. To spice up his Augusta National, Jones had the par fives designed at a distance that could be reached by an aggressive player with two excellent shots.

This was an aspect of the course that Gene had used to his great advantage. He was three under for the tournament at this juncture. But on the par fives to this point, he was 10 under. And the 15th hole had been particularly kind to him, as he had birdied it in each of the three previous rounds. Gene had reached his fair share of the par fives in two this week, but he had not been able to drop an eagle putt and had to settle for two-putt birdies. When he teed off at 15, it would be safe to say he wasn't thinking about a birdie. He wanted eagle.

A straightaway hole, the 15th at that time measured 485 yards. Its fairway falls down a long hillside. A small pond lies between the fairway and the green. Gene's drive was a solid hit with a little draw. Its distance and flight path had it targeted for go-for-it territory. Walter's drive, like his play for this round, was not up to par and short in distance compared to Gene's.

As the two golfers trooped toward their drives, they offered quite the picture in contrast with their caddies. Their keenness for top-notch golf apparel was as strong as it had been during their first showdown in that Unofficial World Championship 13 years earlier. On Gene's bag was Thor Nordwall. On Walter's was Pearly Dawsey. They were members of the Augusta National Caddie Corps, an all-black unit that would be carrying the bags for all Masters contestants until 1983. The two were absent the white overalls that would later become the trademark of their group. They were in very well-worn street clothes and street shoes. Dawsey wore a weathered fedora. Thor Nordwall wore a very distinctive hat, a stovepipe reminiscent of the style worn by Abraham Lincoln. His fondness for this hat had earned him the nickname Stovepipe.

When Gene and Stovepipe arrived at Gene's ball, they were dismayed at what they saw. The drive that had looked so promising when it rocketed off the tee had turned sour. Instead of being situated on top of the grass, Gene's ball had settled down below the grass onto the turf. The hole's layout required a second shot from a downhill lie, but now Gene had to factor in not only the downhill aspect of the swing but its tight lie as well.

While Gene and Stovepipe huddled over the strategy for the next shot, Walter laid his second shot up short of the pond.

A downhill lie was not a situation that caused Gene any pause, because his golf swing had been born on a downhill lie. Some 25 years earlier, Gene had struck his first golf shot on a golf course from a downhill lie. He was three weeks into his days as a caddie and was on the bag of one of the slowest walking and playing members of the club. On one hole that required a blind tee shot, Gene had given his club member his driver, and then scampered up to the crest of the hill to track his tee shot.

Once the member had hit his drive, Gene calculated it would be several minutes for the member to reach the crest of the hill. He hurriedly slipped down the hill until he was out of sight. Then he reached in the pocket of the member's bag and pulled out a ball. Then he grabbed a club from the bag, a jigger, which in the club selections of that day was the equivalent to today's 4-iron. He took his stance and let it rip. To his amazement, he made solid contact and the ball took off with zip and reached the green, coming to rest about 10 feet from the hole.

As a result of this first shot, Gene developed quite an affinity for the jigger. A jigger was in his bag on this day at Augusta, even though it had long been discontinued by golf club manufacturers. It was his go-to club from 175 yards. He would have no doubt loved to have been in its range on this day, but he was some 50 yards outside of its reach.

Gene and Stovepipe weighed the lie and the distance. They both were in agreement that a 3-wood would not get the ball up from its tight lie on the turf. As fate would have it, there was a new addition to Gene's bag from his longtime sponsor, the Wilson Sporting Goods Company. This new addition, given the situation, had a very appropriate name: the Turf Rider. It was not yet available for sale, as a patent for it had been applied for in May 1934. Gene had been given a prototype. It had a hollow-back sole design that allowed it to go down after a ball in a tight lie.

Although the Turf Rider had the design needed to launch the shot, Gene was concerned that the distance the shot needed to carry might be just beyond the club's maximum range. To give it some extra yardage he decided he would close the face of the club slightly. This would decrease the shot's altitude, but hopefully give it the carry it would need.

Gene addressed his ball and took a look at his target. Up until the early 1960s, patrons were allowed to stand behind the green, and there were a half-dozen or so in that position and another half-dozen along the sides. In this group were a few patrons and several others who were in a working capacity. The remaining witnesses that would compose the two dozen who would witness the greatest shot in golf history were scattered along the sides of the fairway. Bobby Jones had reached his observation point, while Stovepipe and Gene were conferring on the shot. One of the last witnesses to take up a position, just moments before Gene took his club back, was a future five-time winner of major championships, including two Masters titles. He was 23-year-old Byron Nelson. Byron, like Gene, was making his first Masters appearance. He had teed off in the group ahead of Gene and Walter. The 17th fairway runs parallel to the 15th. Byron's drive on that hole had strayed into the right rough. As he was approaching his ball, he saw Gene preparing to hit and stopped in his tracks.

From Bobby Jones's viewpoint, Gene's swing looked perfect. By Gene's account, he rode into the shot with everything he had. From the moment of impact, Gene knew it would have enough zip to carry the pond. Its flight path was low, but it was tracking right at the pin. Gene began walking toward the hole. During its five or six seconds in flight, Gene's pace quickened when it struck the ground on the far side of the pond and began to roll onto the green. Gene did not think it would reach the area of the cup but it kept rolling, as if it was being drawn by a magnet, and disappeared into the cup. When it did, with the Turf Rider still in his hand, Gene broke into a full sprint for the green.

Although they were ultra-thin in numbers, the collective whoops and hollers from those around the green easily carried 600 yards to alert the lion's share of the gallery that was still present and congregated around the 18th green that something big had happened. How extraordinarily big would take a few more minutes to be discerned.

As Gene raced onto the green to retrieve his ball from the cup, he passed a young lad whose job it was to radio the clubhouse with scores of players at both the 15th and 16th holes. Those monitoring the radio in the clubhouse received the boy's transmission, but did not believe what he was saying. The lad was obviously mixed up. Sarazen must have made a two at the 145-yard 16th, not the 485-yard 15th. It took several exchanges between the radio operator at the 15th green and the base station in the clubhouse before it was accepted that Gene had, in fact, holed out for a two at the 15th. In mere seconds, the news swept through the clubhouse and out to the gallery around the 18th green. Upon hearing the news, many of them began streaming down toward the 16th hole to follow Gene home.

The Woods were cast aside like yesterday's newspaper. Craig went to the locker room and then out to the 18th green. Jacqueline, now looking drained and anxious, chose to stay close by the radio base station in the clubhouse.

In his phenomenal final round of 1986, Jack Nicklaus dropped what turned out to be the winning stroke at the 17th green. It was a crucial 11-foot putt. As Nicklaus gloriously walked toward the cup to recover his ball, he covered the short distance with his putter held high like a scepter. This scene was seen by millions in television that day and in replays by countless millions since. Still shots of Jack with his putter held high in that moment have also been published in great abundance. Gene covered most of the 235 yards from where he struck his Turf Rider to the green with that club held in his right hand. Unfortunately, there were no newsreel cameras rolling or still photographers to capture the moment.

In discussing all the hoopla about the shot on its 50th anniversary, Gene wasn't lamenting the number who saw the shot. He felt the most interesting aspect of the shot was who was in that select few who did: his archrival, the great Walter Hagen; and the greatest of the great, Bobby Jones.

Jones spoke about that moment often. He had been responsible for the creation of golf's greatest stage, and Gene's shot had placed the Augusta National and the Masters tournament on the map. One last tweak Jones made to his stage set up Gene's moment—the reversing of the nines after the 1934 Masters. Had the 15th hole been played as the sixth that day, it is doubtful Gene would have attempted the shot, given the lie and the fact that there would have been so much more golf left to play.

One other matter is worth mentioning, and that was the parting of ways between Gene and Joe Kirkwood over the pricing of the admission to their exhibitions in New Zealand. Had this not occurred, Gene likely would have taken another pass on the Masters and would have been touring with Joe in Japan in April 1935.

After waiting for Walter to complete his play of the 15th, Gene, now in a tie with Wood, walked briskly to the par-three 16th tee. This hole played at only 145 yards in 1935. Gene's tee shot left him 10 feet from the hole. His putt for birdie was way too strong, and he had to sink a knee-knocker coming back to save his par. At the par-four 17th Gene put his approach into the middle of the green. His first putt was more of a lag roll than a serious birdie attempt, and he tapped in for par.

The doglegged par-four 18th at 420 yards, requiring an approach shot that was uphill, was quite the test by 1935 standards, which made Craig Wood's closing birdie all the more impressive. To make a winning birdie here, Gene needed a big drive. He didn't get it. Where he had hoped to use a 5- or 6-iron to get home, Gene's distance to the green again required him to grab the Turf Rider from his bag. There was a stiff breeze coming from the left. Gene aimed for the green's left edge, anticipating the wind would bring it back to the hole. That aspect of the shot went as planned.

But the Turf Rider brought the ball in too hot, and it rolled well past the pin.

Gene was left with a treacherous downhill putt. He wanted to put a good roll on it for a birdie that would give him the victory, but the possibility of losing it all with a three-putt also weighed on his mind. He surveyed the putt from every angle. Given that it was a steep downhiller, one couldn't blame Gene for being a little cautious with his stroke. But he was too cautious. His putt, as Gene described it, "died a slow death." When it was pronounced dead, it rested three feet above the hole. Groans and murmurs resonated from the gallery packed around the green. A three-footer above the hole on an Augusta National green typically is handled with the kind of study and caution a bomb squad would employ when disarming an intricate explosive device. Throw in the fact that this three-footer was needed to remain tied and force a play-off, and the pressure meter was off the charts.

Although one can imagine all sorts of pressure on the inside, Gene's outward appearance and actions defied the moment. He walked down the sloping green and, without any study or second of deliberation, drilled the putt into the back of the cup.

Gene and Craig Wood faced off in a 36-hole play-off the next day. After having victory snatched from him in such a specular fashion, not many observers were giving Craig much of chance. They teed off in near-freezing temperatures, and Craig grabbed an early lead. But when they reached the turn the temperature had warmed, Gene had rallied, and they were tied. At the 10th green, Gene drained a 20-foot birdie to take the lead. Over the next 24 holes, Gene ran off all pars while Craig was making a cluster of bogeys. At one point early on the back nine of the second 18, Gene was leading by eight strokes. Wood shaved three strokes off that margin on the closing holes. The final count for the day was Sarazen, 144, and Wood, 149.

At the conclusion of the play-off, Grantland Rice served as the master of ceremonies at the awards presentation. He presented the winner's check of $1,500 to Gene. Gene made some brief remarks, in which he credited the Augusta National as being one of the finest courses in the world, and stated that he believed its tournament was on par with the National Open in the amount of interest it generated and in its level of competition.

15

POST-SHOT

A few days after his playoff with Wood, Gene wrote an article for the Associated Press that was carried in the *New York Times*, detailing his win at Augusta and his plans for taking dead aim at the U.S. Open in June at Oakmont. In it he wrote, "I recall that [Bobby] Jones won [the Southeastern Open] here in Augusta before starting his grand slam sweep in 1930. I hope it is a good omen for me."

The field at Oakmont would be facing a much different course than the one faced when the club last hosted the Open back in 1927. The course that had been considered one of the toughest tests in American golf had been made even tougher with the altering of 12 holes to make them even more challenging. For the 1927 Open, Oakmont boasted 150 sand traps; for the 1935 Open, players would find that number increased to 182.

Between Augusta and Oakmont, Gene spent a considerable amount of time working on his sand game. As the golfer who had "fired the shot heard 'round the world," there were abundant opportunities for Gene to cash in. One of these allowed him to get paid while working on his sand game. This opportunity was not at a golf course, but in a grand glass-and-marble structure at the corner of 7th and F Street in Washington, DC, Hecht's Department Store.

A large chain of department stores that operated mainly in the Mid-Atlantic states, Hecht's flagship store was its Washington, DC, location. Hecht's retained Gene's services on a Saturday one month before the Open to give a talk about golf, and the store had a sand trap constructed for Gene to demonstrate bunker shots into a net. Gene put on two two-hour sessions to overflow crowds. In these sessions, he went over the ABCs of golf, demonstrated sand shots, and fielded questions from the audience. He also talked at length about his "shot heard 'round the world" and held up the Turf Rider he had used for all to see.

Gene also showed the crowds a new club he had helped develop that he felt was going to improve his chances at Oakmont—an 8 ½-iron.

A few days before the Open began, Gene had been asked to comment on Walter Hagen's chances. Gene said it was his opinion that it would be like thinking the winner of the 1915 Kentucky Derby could win the 1935 Kentucky Derby.

When the final round had begun at Oakmont, three shots separated the top eight players on the leaderboard. Gene was one of them, and so was that old nag, Walter. Among this eight, Gene and Walter were the last to tee off. Gene's time was 15 minutes ahead of Walter's. Three shots back, Gene suffered a huge setback at the first hole when he opened with a double bogey and never recovered.

Walter, on the other hand, was far from done. Between the sand traps and the super-quick greens, scoring on the refortified Oakmont had proven to be a formidable exercise. Only two players in the field had broken par all week, and that was by one stroke. Walter toured the front side in even par, and when he stepped on the 10th tee, he was on the cusp of adding a 12th major title to his resume. If he could play Oakmont's back side in even par he would best the leader, Sam Parks Jr., a 25-year-old local Pittsburgh-area professional who had never won a tournament. But it wasn't in the cards. Walter ran out of gas coming down the stretch. He bogeyed four holes in a row to finish in a tie for third, four strokes behind the winner, Parks.

Gene finished in sixth place, but he could take some solace playing a part in Parks's success. When Gene was working at the Highland Country Club back in 1922, he had given the then 13-year-old Parks his first golf lesson.

Although the 8 ½-iron Gene introduced at Oakmont never caught on, he did play an unwitting part in the development of a device that is used extensively today in preparing greens for tournament play—the Stipmeter. Its inventor was Edward Stimpson, who was an accomplished golfer in his own right. He had recently won the Massachusetts state amateur championship, and had served as captain of the Harvard University golf team. One of many facets that made Oakmont then and now so challenging is its lighting-fast greens. Stimpson was in the gallery at the 1935 Open and witnessed a putt of Gene's roll off the green and into a bunker. Seeing Gene's ball speed across the green was the moment when Stimpson saw the need for a way to measure the speed of a green, and he went about the task of developing the Stipmeter. He came up with an angled track that releases a ball at a known velocity so that the distance it rolls on a green's surface can be measured. It would take a while before its use became standard practice at tournaments, but that began in 1976 when the USGA began using an updated version at that year's Open.

There was a tight window that year between the British Open and the U.S. Open. The ship Gene wanted to take left the New York City harbor at midnight on the day the U.S. Open ended. To get there in time, Gene would have had to fly from Pittsburgh to New York City immediately after the conclusion of play at Oakmont. This was something he did not want to do. Later sailings would not provide him with what he considered ample time to get rid of his sea legs and to practice, so he decided to skip the British Open.

While the focus of the golf world was on the run-up to and the play of the British Open, Gene picked up two wins. The first was the Long Island Open, a 36-hole, one day event; the second was the Massachusetts Open. In late September, Gene made a strong showing in the 1935 Ryder Cup at the Ridgewood Country Club in Paramus, New Jersey, won by the U.S. team nine and three. The team again was captained by Walter Hagen. On the first day, Gene teamed with Walter in the foursome matches and they routed their British counterparts—Alf Perry, who had won the 1935 British Open, and Jackson Busson—seven and six. In the singles the next day, Gene took the measure of Busson, three and two.

In the PGA Championship at Twin Hills Golf and Country Club in Oklahoma City, Oklahoma, Gene again fell victim to a young upstart professional. His name was Butch Krueger and he hailed from Beloit, Wisconsin. Krueger was a golf professional by day and a semipro baseball pitcher by night. He had played in the U.S. Open at Oakmont, and in the first round shot one of the only two subpar rounds of the tournament. He was one of the four players who had finished in a four-way tie with Gene for sixth place.

Gene and Butch met in the third round, and it was a nip-and-tuck affair. They were all square thorough 13 holes. Back-to-back bogeys then put Gene two down with three to go. The 16th hole was halved. At the 17th green, both had birdie putts. Butch went first and left his six inches from the cup. Gene also missed. His ball stopped two inches from the hole and directly in the path of Butch's putt for par. Gene was not required to mark his ball, as the stymie rule was still on the books. Krueger would have to go around it or over it. He chose the latter. He gave Gene a cocky smile and then chipped his ball over Gene's into the cup to halve the hole and take the match two up with one to go.

As the last weeks of 1935 were winding down, the man who had struck the most famous shot in golf history nine months earlier was not feeling good about his swing, so Gene journeyed down to Pinehurst, North Carolina, to have his swing checked out. The man he went to see wasn't a touring pro or a noted instructor. He was one of two brothers who had interceded on Gene's behalf and had put a little member pressure on the Brooklawn Golf Club professional, George Sparling, to give Gene a shot as his pro shop attendant/club maker/janitor. His name was Archie Wheeler. Archie, now in his early 70s, was a man of significant means. In his younger years, he had played amateur golf on a high level. While Gene was at Brooklawn, he had played a substantial amount of golf with Archie. The two had developed a strong bond and had remained close over the 16 years since they met.

Archie liked to spend a good bit of time at Pinehurst in the winter. Gene sought him out there, and the men spent two hours together at a practice area known as "maniac hill." Dave Herman with the *Washington Post* heard about Gene and Archie's session. He contacted Gene, then wrote a short piece about it. The piece included the following quote from Gene: "When I get a little off, Wheeler can tell in a minute what I am doing wrong."

The Agua Caliente five-year run as golf's richest event ended after the 1935 tournament, when the Mexican government banned gambling and the resort closed. The Masters was now the unquestioned biggest event of the 1936 winter tour. In the run-up for its third edition, you would have expected that Gene, defending champion, or one of several others in the tour's top tier would be the favorite. But the favorite spot was given to the event's host, Bobby Jones. Despite his flat performances in the first two Masters, the super-strong aura of his accomplishments was the primary fuel for his standing, along with reports that he had put in the same practice regimen he had used for major championships in his heyday.

Also, he would have something in his bag this time that had been missing in the previous two Masters: the original Calamity Jane, the putter he had made famous.

On day one of the Masters, Bobby and Gene were the marquee pairing. They were the last to go off, and with them was most of the gallery. It did not go well for the greatest golfer the game had ever known, or for the man who had hit the shot heard 'round the world. Bobby made bogey on the first four holes, missing putts of four feet or less on three of them. Gene's bogeys were spread out over the 18 holes. At the end of the round, both players had posted rounds of six-over-par 78.

On day two, Bobby again posted a 78 to kill any chances of a strong showing. Gene, on the other hand, bounced back in a big way. Spurred by a birdie on the par-three sixth and an eagle on the par-five eighth, Gene shot a five-under-par round of 67 to finish the day in the fourth spot. His 67 equaled the tournament record set the year before by Henry Picard. Gene was not alone in shooting a record-tying 67 that day. He was joined by the man he had snatched the Masters title from the year before, Craig Wood. Gene's and Bobby's poor performances on the first day paled in comparison to what Craig had experienced: he had shot an 88 in his first round.

Rain forced a 36-hole finish on Monday; many believed it should have been a Tuesday finish, as most of those last two rounds were played in high wind and in off-and-on deluges. Gene started the last round seven strokes back, but he put on quite a kick over the last 18 holes. He shot a 70, which was one of only two subpar rounds posted over the final 18 holes. At the end of the day he came up short, finishing in third, two strokes behind the winner, Horton Smith.

At the U.S. Open in early June at Baltusrol Golf Club in Springfield, New Jersey, Gene's play was off in the first two rounds, and it was obvious to him that it was not his week. For the 36-hole final day, he requested to be paired with Tony Manero, a close friend who was in contention. At this time there was still no formal structure for pairings and requests of this kind were often granted, and the USGA saw fit to grant Gene's request. Manero was a fellow Italian American, and was especially high-strung. Gene believed he kept Manero calm during the last two rounds. After the morning 18, Tony was four strokes off the lead. He caught fire in the afternoon session and shot a 67 to nose out Harry Cooper by one stroke for the title.

Some who had witnessed the interactions between Tony and Gene during those last two rounds were of the opinion that Gene had stepped across the line from encouraging his playing partner to actually advising him, a violation of the rules, and a complaint was filed with the USGA. The USGA officials huddled for almost an hour, going over the charges, before they ruled that there was no evidence of wrongdoing.

There was a three-week window between the U.S. Open and the British Open. Gene opted to make the journey across the Atlantic. Interest among American professionals in the Open Championship was waning. Gene was the only U.S. professional of note to make the trip. Royal Liverpool at Hoylake was the host venue. Gene was in the hunt from the opening round until his putter let him down on the final nine. He finished in a four-way tie for fifth place, four strokes behind the winner, Alf Padgham.

Gene returned to the States for just a few weeks, and then he and wife Mary set sail for another tour of New Zealand and Australia. Accompanying them on the trip was the 1931 Women's U.S. Amateur champion, Helen Hicks. In 1934, Hicks had turned professional when she signed on with Gene's longtime sponsor, the Wilson Sporting Goods Company, to assist in the further development of the company's line of women's golf equipment. While on this tour, Gene and Helen would play in exhibition matches almost daily.

While in Australia, Gene took some time off from exhibition matches to take part in the Australian Open in late September at the Metropolitan Golf Club in Melbourne. He won the event by four strokes, becoming the first American ever to claim that crown.

The year 1936 did not end well for Gene. The PGA Championship was held in mid-November at Pinehurst No. 2. Gene returned from Australia just in time to make the event, but he wasn't there long. In the first round, he fell victim again to a virtual unknown. This time it was Jack Patroni, who was a club pro in Delaware. The match went the full 18 holes with Patroni squeaking out a one-up win.

Over the remaining years of the 1930s, Gene had three wins but none came in a significant event. He had a couple of top-10 finishes at the Masters. He made one trip across the Atlantic to play in the 1937 Ryder Cup at the Southport and Ainsdale Golf Club in Southport, England, and the 1937 British Open at Carnoustie Golf Links in Carnoustie, Scotland. The United States took the Ryder Cup in an eight to four win, marking the first time a host team had failed to win the competition. Gene and partner Denny Shute halved their foursome match on day one. In the singles matches the following day, Gene edged Percy Allis one-up. Two weeks later at the British Open at Carnoustie, Gene played poorly and missed the cut.

As the summer of 1939 was winding down, anticipation for the 1939 Ryder Cup, to be played in November at the Ponte Verda Golf Club in Jacksonville, Florida, was building. Walter Hagen was again named the American team's captain. Henry Cotton, the winner of the 1934 and 1937 British Opens, would lead the team from Great Britain. The British were anxious to avenge their defeat in 1937, so much so that Charles Roe, the head of the British PGA, had issued an edict that the wives of the players would not be allowed to make the trip. As part of his justification for this decision, Rose cited Gene and Walter Hagen. They had been critical of their Ryder Cup teammates who had brought their wives to the 1937 Ryder Cup at Southport, as they believed the women's presence had been an undue distraction to their husbands.

When it came time to pick his team for Ponte Verda, Captain Hagen had the most talented group ever from which to make his selections. A number of high-profile players would not make the team. Gene was one of them, and he was incensed. As it turned out, there would be no Ryder Cup at Ponte Verda anyway. In early September, Britain formally declared it was at war with Germany. The Ryder Cup was cancelled the next day, and its play would not resume until 1947.

Prior to the 1940 U.S. Open at the Canterbury Golf Club outside of Cleveland, the only events of note for Gene was a tie for 21st at the Masters and his participation in a unique golf experiment. As demonstrated by his enlarging-the-cup idea, Gene was always ready to push the envelope. In this case, he was going to participate in an exhibition match in Norwalk, Connecticut, with Jimmy Demaret, the winner of the 1940 Masters, and two high-profile amateurs, heavyweight boxing great Gene Tunney and Babe Ruth. In this exhibition, the only thing they would be guaranteed was room to swing the club. The gallery was going to be practically on top of them and could hoop, holler, and cheer to their hearts content.

The event was staged to benefit a local hospital, and a crowd estimated at 5,000 showed up and was abundantly raucous. To add even more commotion, there was a sound truck blaring out what could be loosely called music, and a small group of musicians that stayed as close to the golfers as possible, playing with as much vigor as possible. Gene, who had always believed that a good golfer should no more be affected by noise than a major league baseball player performing on the diamond, shot one over par. Demaret was even par on that day. Ruth seemed to handle the noise well. Tunney did struggle from time to time, which he attributed to not enough recent time on the course.

Demaret and Ruth were playing partners and they won the match, defeating Tunney and Gene two-up with one to go. Ruth got the laugh of the day. When Tunney dribbled a drive 40 yards off the tee, Ruth told him he should run it out anyway.

In his sectional qualifier for the 1940 U.S. Open, which was returning that year to the Canterbury Golf Club near Cleveland, Gene was in the middle of the pack of those who qualified. When he reached Canterbury, nobody was giving him much of a chance. Among those in the know, his name could not be found on their list of favorites. The lion's share of the smart money was being placed on Sam Snead. He was not only the oddsmaker's favorite; Sam was the sentimental favorite as well, due to what had occurred at the previous year's Open at the Philadelphia Country Club. When he reached the par-five 18th tee in the final round, Sam knew he was in the hunt, but the absence of leaderboards at that time placed him in the dark as to how he exactly stood. News of what was going on worked its way through the crowd, so when a spectator in the gallery at the 18th tee told Sam he needed a birdie to win, he believed it.

But Sam had received bad intelligence—a bogey would result in a play-off, par and he would be the winner. Sam played the hole aggressively. He found a bunker with his second shot. His third shot stayed in the bunker. With his fourth shot, he airmailed the green. Once on in five, he three-putted for an eight that dropped him to fifth place. Byron Nelson, Craig Wood, and Denny Shute finished in a three-way tie at the end of regulation. Nelson won the 18-hole play-off the next day.

At Canterbury, the smart money seemed to be well placed. Sam Snead opened with a 67 for the first-round lead. After round two he was sharing the lead with two others. But with 36 holes scheduled for the last day, things could get really turned around, and they did. Sam started the final round one shot out of the lead. His final 18 would be very painful. Instead of seeing it all go up in smoke on one hole as it did the year before, it was an excruciatingly long afternoon of bogey after bogey that saw him post a final-round score of 81 and drop him all the way down to a 16th-place finish.

As the second 18 of the day moved into its final stages, Lawson Little was the leader in the clubhouse. There was only one golfer still out on the course who had a shot at catching him, and he was Gene. Like he had done at Skokie in 1922 and at Fresh Meadow in 1932, Gene was making a charge on the last day. He had stayed in or around the top 10 for the first two rounds and moved up into fifth after round three with a two-under-par 70, one of only a handful of players who bested par in that 18. What had been keeping Gene hanging around the leaders the first two rounds and had thrust him into contention in round three on the last day was a gift from Archie Wheeler, his longtime friend, supporter, and sometimes instructor. Around the turn of the century, Archie and his brother were into amateur golf in a big way. They were often at big amateur events in the Mideast and were friends with the country's top amateur, Walter Travis. When they would attend these tournaments, the brothers felt obliged to purchase clubs from the pro shop of the host venue as a way of lending support to that club and its professional.

Two weeks before the Open at Canterbury, Archie met up with Gene and gave him a putter from one of those purchases from some 40 years ago. Gene tried out the putter and took a liking to it and decided to put it in his bag for the Open.

Gene was two off the lead when he started his final back nine. On the 10th, he was in danger of dropping another stroke behind, but Archie's putter really caught fire at this point, as Gene dropped a 12-footer to save his par. At the par-three 11th hole, he dropped another 12-footer for birdie to pull within one of the lead. On 12, it was a 10-footer to save par. He gave his putter an easy putt for birdie at 13 to pull even with Lawson Little. Gene picked up a tap-in par at 14 and rolled in a 12-footer for another par at 15. Sixteen was a par courtesy of a knee-knocker from seven feet.

The situation became really sticky at the par-three 17th. Gene missed the green and then skulled a chip shot 30 feet past the hole. He was faced with a downhill curling putt to save his par. Gene gave it the right line and right pace, and it dropped into the dead center of the cup to keep him tied with Lawson Little.

At the par-four 18th, Gene's approach caught the far right side of the green, leaving him a 50-foot birdie putt for the win. As it had at Fresh

Meadow back in 1932, security around the 18th green broke down, and the gallery surged onto the left side of the green. It took several minutes for them to be cleared and order restored. If this putt had dropped, it would have been quite the storybook finish, but it wasn't to be. Gene's putt singed the right side of the cup before coming to a stop two inches behind it.

Gene and Lawson had an 18-hole play-off the following day. Little took the lead at the first hole and never relinquished it. He consistently outdrove Gene by 20 to 30 yards, and his approach game and putting was a model of consistency. At the end of the round, Lawson was the winner by three strokes. It could have been worse, if it had not been for Archie's putter. Gene rolled in a 60-foot putt for eagle on the sixth hole and a 35-footer for birdie at the 11th.

When it was over, it was hard to say who had taken the defeat harder, Gene or the lion's share of the gallery that had been rooting for him. When Lawson tapped in his final putt at 18, he received only a smattering of applause.

Back in the summer of 1939, when Gene was seething about being left off the Ryder Cup team, he had thrown down a challenge: that he could pick a team from the other top names in professional golf who had not made the squad and defeat the Ryder Cup squad. Since Britain's entry into World War II had cancelled the Ryder Cup matches, it was decided that the American team should showcase its talents in a match, and the PGA took up Gene on his challenge. It was announced a few days after the 1940 U.S. Open that the Ryder Cup team would face off against Gene's team in a fund-raiser for the Red Cross. The match would take place in a little over a month at Walter Hagen's old home course, the Oakland Hills Country Club outside of Detroit.

On the eve of the matches, Gene and Walter sat down to iron out the particulars of the match. At the 72nd hole at the Open at Canterbury, when Gene was lining up that 50-foot putt that would have won the event, Walter was standing in the gallery nearby and voiced some encouraging words. On this occasion, the two just had words. When Gene could not get Walter to agree to several particulars on the match he was proposing, things got heated and ended up with Gene storming out of the room. In an Associated Press story carried in the *Washington Post* the following day, it was reported that after their verbal brouhaha Walter said, "That's why he never was captain of the team. He couldn't sit down and get something like this ironed out." The top names on Hagen's Ryder Cup team were Byron Nelson, Sam Snead, Horton Smith, and Paul Runyan. Gene's team featured Jimmy Demaret, Ben Hogan, Tommy Armour, and Lawson Little. In the foursome matches on day one, Gene's team put themselves in a hole, losing three of the four matches.

In the singles competition the next day, the matches were split four and four, which gave Hagen's team a seven to five victory and left Gene clamoring for a rematch.

In late March 1941, Gene took part in another high-profile exhibition to benefit the Red Cross. This one took place in Nassau in the Bahamas. The United States would not officially enter World War II until after the attack on Pearl Harbor in the coming December. This Nassau event was for the Red Cross's efforts in Great Britain. The host of the event was the former Prince of Wales, who now carried the title of the Duke of Windsor. He had given up the throne as king of England in 1936 to marry Wallis Simpson and was now serving as the governor of the Bahamas.

Dubbed the "Match of Champions," it was arguably the most illustrious event of its kind ever staged, as it featured—along with Gene, Bobby Jones, Walter Hagen, and Tommy Armour—the Duke of Windsor as referee. Walter and Gene put aside their Ryder Cup differences and teamed up against Jones and Armour. The match was broadcast on radio back in the States. It took place over two days with 18 holes being played each day. Jones and Armour were victorious, taking a three and two decision.

Several weeks later at the 1941 Masters, Craig Wood, who had lost in the play-offs at the British Open, the U.S. Open, the PGA, and to Gene in the 1935 Masters, finally came home the winner. Ironically, his key moment would come on his second shot at the same 15th hole where Gene had erased his three-stroke deficit with one shot. Craig had to be thinking that things were about to unravel on him again. He had just bogeyed 14 and was clinging to a one-stroke lead over Byron Nelson, who was in the group behind him. To add a little more pressure to a situation that didn't need any more, it had been Byron who had beaten him in a play-off in the 1939 U.S. Open.

Wood's drive at 15 had left him about the same distance from the hole as Gene had been in 1935. The safe play would have been to take the pond in front of the green out of play and to lay up. But Craig decided not to play it safe. He asked his caddie for his 3-wood and then gave it a ride.

The shot easily cleared the pond, and Craig two-putted for birdie. The momentum he picked up at 15 carried over to 16. He picked up another birdie there while Byron had to settle for par at 15, and suddenly Craig had a three-shot lead. He parred in to win by that number.

In that 1941 Masters, Gene finished in a tie for 19th. Two months later, he finished in a tie for seventh in the U.S. Open at the Colonial Country Club in Fort Worth. It would be his last high finish in that event. The winner, who was 10 strokes ahead of Gene, was putting some more distance between him and his bridesmaid tag. It was Craig Wood.

There was much hype going into the PGA Championship at the Cherry Hills Country Club in Denver about the prospect of Wood becoming the first player to win the Masters, the U.S. Open, and the PGA in the same year. Those prospects died an early death, as Wood was eliminated in the round of 32. Gene made what would turn out to be his last big push for a major win in the event, making it all the way to the semifinals before falling to Byron Nelson two and one.

16

GOLF'S AMBASSADOR

A few days after Pearl Harbor, the USGA cancelled its events until the end of World War II. The PGA soon followed suit. The Masters went on as scheduled in April 1942. Byron Nelson defeated Ben Hogan in an 18-hole play-off to claim his second Masters title. Gene was never a factor in this one. He shot an 80 in the first round and ended up finishing in a tie for 28th place.

After the 1942 event, the Masters tournament joined the other two American majors in suspending its play until the end of the war. The PGA tour played a limited schedule of events for most of the next three years. Gene was active in supporting the country's war effort during this period. He took part in countless exhibitions to raise funds for the USO, the Red Cross, and for the purchase of war bonds. He also made several extended tours of military bases, putting on clinics and playing in exhibitions to entertain the troops. One of those stops was the training base at Parris Island, South Carolina, where several thousand Marines followed Gene as he played a match on the base's course.

After the war ended and golf returned to its full schedule, Gene was in his twilight years as far as being a serious contender. There were a few flourishes, but for the most part he had transitioned to the role of sentimental favorite. One of those flourishes came in May 1948, at the PGA Championship at the Norwood Hills Country Club in St. Louis. Gene, now 46 years old, won his first two matches to make it to the round of 16 where he faced Ben Hogan, the hottest golfer in the game. Deep into the 36-hole match it appeared to be a cakewalk for Ben. Gene was five down, but put together a furious closing rally. When they reached the final green, Gene had a 30-foot birdie putt to tie the match. Ben managed to escape with a one-up win as Gene's putt grazed the hole but would not drop.

A month later, Hogan would win the 1948 U.S. Open at Riviera Country Club in Pacific Palisades, becoming the first player to equal Gene's feat of 26 years earlier, winning both the U.S. Open and the PGA Championship in the same year.

Just before the 1950 Masters, Gene's book, *Thirty Years of Championship Golf* that he penned with the assistance of Herbert Warren Wind, was released. Priced at $2.50, patrons of that year's Masters could purchase a copy at a table near the first tee. In the Masters, Gene turned in a very respectable performance, coming back from an opening round of 80 to finish in 10th place.

In the late 1940s, Gene began to expand his role as the unofficial go-to guy for commentary on the state of the game. Often, he would actually be the one to trigger a discussion or stir up a debate. After his opening round in 1950 at Augusta, Gene got fired up about one of his pet peeves—slow play. He had been paired with Jimmy Demaret. Teeing off six minutes behind them was the pairing of Frank Stranahan, one of the country's top amateurs, and Joe Kirkwood's son, Joe Kirkwood Jr. Young Kirkwood was one of the more unique participants in the Masters—not only was he a professional golfer, he was an actor as well.

In 1930s, the comic strip Joe Palooka, about a heavyweight boxing champion, made its debut and it was soon being carried in over 900 newspapers. In the late 1940s Monogram Pictures brought the strip to the silver screen and cast Joe Jr. as Palooka. He would play Palooka in 12 hour-length films, and would later play Palooka in a television series in the mid-1950s.

When Gene and Jimmy finished their opening round, it was brought to Gene's attention that the pairing of Frank Stranahan and Joe Jr., who should have been preparing to play their approach shots on 18 as soon as Jimmy and Gene had exited the green, were in fact only now playing the 15th hole. This sent Gene into a tirade over slow play in the locker room. He bemoaned the snail's pace of the game's current crop of young players, who seemingly wanted everything but a meteorologist report before playing their next shot. Shirley Povich devoted much of his report from the Masters for the *Washington Post* to Gene's rant, including the aspect that was most upsetting to Gene—how slow play by the pros was bleeding into the play of the average golfer. Gene summed up his frustration in the following statement: "They got every 100-shooter in the country going into the same kind of clinical study and soliloquy because they think it is fashionable?"

As one would have expected, Gene's opining could often get under the skin of his fellow professionals. A month after the 1950 Masters, Jimmy Demaret, his playing partner in that first round at Augusta, went after Gene for his constant criticism in an interview with a United Press International reporter. Jimmy claimed that Gene never said anything good about golf, always running down the game and its players—a game that had given him a chance to make a fortune.

What had set Jimmy off were recent comments Gene had made about Sam Snead not wanting to compete in the British Open because of the cost, a factor that often weighed heavily on Gene's mind when he was making trips across the Atlantic to compete in the same event. Gene suggested that Sam owed it to the game to make the trip and threw in this comment, reported by the Associated Press: "If it wasn't for golf, Sam Snead would be shining shoes in White Sulphur Springs, West Virginia." In his tirade, carried in the *Washington Post*, Jimmy asserted that if it wasn't for golf then Gene would be on a banana boat between Sicily and Naples.

Asked for a response on Jimmy's comments, Gene said they left him unperturbed except for one, and that was Jimmy's remark about the banana boat.

Less than a year later, Demaret became embroiled in a big controversy, and Gene was quick to take a side and jump into the fray. Given their most recent history of verbal jousting, one would have assumed Gene would have taken the opposite side in the brouhaha, but that was not the case. Gene was one of the first and one of the most vocal in springing to Jimmy's defense. This was not a case of Gene wanting to bury the hatchet. It was the case of Gene desiring to put a hatchet in the other side of the controversy—the PGA, which was a foe of Gene's at a much higher level than Jimmy would ever reach.

Demaret and three other lesser-known players had skipped the Rio Grande Valley Open in Harlingen, Texas, to play in the Mexican Open. The PGA allowed players to skip their events, provided the event they were taking part in was a major championship. The PGA did not recognize the Mexican Open as a major and imposed fines on Demaret—who finished seventh in Mexico, 12 strokes behind the winner, Roberto De Vicenzo—and the three lesser-known PGA members who had played in the tournament.

Gene believed that, although it would be a stretch to give major status to the Mexican Open, the PGA should have recognized that by banning the players from participating they were belittling Mexico and stirring up bad feelings. Gene's bad-blood relationship with the PGA had started with the controversy over the omission of Billy Burke from the 1933 Ryder Cup team and the scheduling snafu over the 1933 PGA Championship, and had been building ever since. Gene's favorite refrain about the PGA was "when did they ever do anything smart."

Their actions in the Mexican Open/Demaret flap would more than support Gene's refrain. They fined Demaret $500 and the three lesser-known players only $200 each. It is likely they chose to hit Demaret harder because it was known he had received appearance money and had his expenses paid for playing in the Mexican Open.

Demaret refused to pay the fine and was sabre-rattling that he intended to sue the PGA. The timing of the situation could not have been worse for the PGA. The next event on the schedule was the Housten Open. Demaret's popularity there was through the roof. Houston was his hometown. He wasn't backing down about paying the fine, and the PGA was sticking to its guns. The Mexican standoff ended when a Texas oil magnate, Glenn McCarthy, stepped in and not only paid Demaret's fine but that of the three lesser-known players as well.

Over the next several years, Gene would challenge the way the PGA conducted its business on a number of fronts. He wanted a permanent date set for of the PGA Championship. Over the years, it had been all over the calendar. Most recently, it had been played too close to the U.S. Open. Gene felt this was unfair to a number of players who had to travel great distances in a short period of time. It also resulted in their missing their duties at their home club during the peak time of the year. Gene also wanted the conceding of putts during the PGA Championship eliminated. He cited his own experience in a match in the Championship when he did not concede a 14-inch putt to Byron Nelson, and Nelson missed.

Gene also decided to take the British PGA to task for the way their Ryder Cup team was formulated. He proposed that their team's roster should include players from throughout the British Empire, not just Great

Britain. He also recommended that during the years that the United States hosted the Ryder Cup, it should be played the week before the U.S. Open, so the visiting squad could take part in that event as well.

Over the remainder of the 1950s, Gene experienced both highs and lows at Augusta. In 1951, he followed up his 10th-place finish in 1950 with a 12th place finish. The following year he had a low, as he elected to withdraw after the 12th hole during his opening round, not as the result of an injury but because he was in a state of shock.

Of the 18 holes at Augusta, none was more vexing than the shortest hole among them, the 155-yard, par-three 12th. The hole features the infamous Rae's Creek streaming just in front of its thin green, and plenty of trouble behind it. Since the first Masters, it has humbled the game's biggest names. Jack Nicklaus and Bobby Jones both shanked tee shots there. Tom Weiskopf put five balls in the water in 1980, scoring a 13. The hole always takes on its most treacherous nature in the final round, squashing the hopes and chances of many a Masters contender. In the 2016 Masters, Jordan Spieth appeared to be well on his way to victory in the last round, until he reached the 12th. He put two balls in the creek and ended up with a quadruple bogey seven. He would end up finishing in a tie for second, three strokes behind the winner, Danny Willet.

The 12th hole was responsible for Gene's withdrawal from the 1952 Masters. His opening round had gotten off to a good start and he was one under par when he reached the 12th tee. His tee shot splashed into Rae's Creek. He took a drop and, like Jordon Spieth, that one landed in the water as well. He dropped another ball. This one he sent over the green. From there, he took three more shots to get his ball into the hole for an eight.

In an Associated Press story carried in the *Washington Post*, it was reported that Gene gave this explanation for his withdrawal at the clubhouse later that afternoon: "It was the greatest shock on the golf course I have ever had. I had been hitting the ball so well then to have that happen—I couldn't take it."

Three years later in 1955, on the day before the start of the Masters, it was time to celebrate the 20th anniversary of the most celebrated shot in golf history. To commemorate it, a stone bridge was built across the edge of the pond that fronts the green and was officially named the "Sarazen Bridge."

A crowd of several thousand gathered for its unveiling ceremony, and both Gene and Bobby Jones made brief remarks about that day in 1935. Once the formalities were concluded, Gene walked out to what he estimated to be the spot where he had sent his Turf Rider 4-wood shot rocketing toward the hole and marked it. From there 43 of the players in the field for the 1955 Masters attempted to duplicate the shot. Each player was given two attempts. Only about ten players were able to have their shots clear the pond and stay on the green. The best shot among the 86 attempts belonged to Fred Haas Jr., with a shot that came to rest four feet from the cup. Haas had made his debut at the Masters in 1935 as a 19-year-old amateur and had finished 37th.

Two years later in the 1957 Masters, Gene, for the first time other than by his own choosing, was not around for the weekend as the result of a big change in the tournament's format. In this edition of the tournament, a cut was implemented to reduce the field after 36 holes to the top 40 and ties. A number of reasons were cited for the move, but it was speculated that the chief reason was to make it more expedient for television coverage. The Masters had been televised for the first time the previous year.

Television networks were experiencing growing pains in their golf coverage, so anything that would help them out was a plus. Gene had firsthand experience in that regard. NBC had brought him on board as part of their broadcast team at the 1955 U.S. Open at the Olympic Club in San Francisco. Under heavy time constraints, Gene had signed off the telecast declaring Ben Hogan as the winner. Ben had completed his round and, in a scenario akin to Craig Wood's at Augusta in 1935, he had what was thought to be bullet-proof lead. The problem was that nobody informed Jack Fleck, an unheralded driving range operator from Iowa. Jack was still on his back nine and put on a closing surge to tie Ben. He then beat Ben by three strokes in a play-off the next day.

Gene was opposed to the change. His allegiance was to the fans who were on the grounds. He did not want those in attendance on the weekend to lose the opportunity to see all the greats in the field play. Gene missed the cut. He was not alone; joining him on the sidelines for the weekend were Ben Hogan and the current U.S. Open champion, Cary Middlecoff. Ben had missed the cut off by one stroke, Cary by two, and Gene by five. Gene would be a participant in 15 of the next 16 Masters, but would make the cut only once over that span. It came in 1963, when he was 61 years old.

Qualifying for the 1957 U.S. Open for the metropolitan district of New York took place in White Plains, New York, on June 3. There were 141 players competing for 18 spots. Competing for one of those spots was a 55-year-old named Gene Sarazen. Due to the large field, play was divided between two nearby courses, the Knollwood Country Club and the Metropolis Golf Club, with each player playing one round at each course.

Gene had failed to qualify for 1956 Open, marking the first time since 1920 he had not been in the field. His morning round at Metropolis was two over par, leaving him in a bad spot. His afternoon round was not looking any better; he was coming in three strokes off the projected cut line after completing the 12th hole. But starting at the 13th, he seemingly turned back the clock to his glory days. He birdied five of those last six holes to safely cruise into the top 18 by two strokes.

The 1957 Open was taking place where it had all started for Gene 37 years earlier in 1920, the Inverness Club in Toledo, Ohio. In 1920 the course had measured 6,569 yards. For the 1957 Open it was being stretched out to 6,961 yards. The length of golf courses had been the most recent cause Gene had taken up. He didn't want them any longer. Gene wanted them shorter. He advocated that, when new courses were being built, they should not be more than 5,000 yards in length. The advantages of this plan were that it would reduce construction costs and upkeep, reduce the amount of time required to play a round, and make the game more enjoyable for middle-aged people.

About the only good experience of the 1957 Open would belong to Dick Mayer, who would take home the trophy by defeating defending champion Cary Middlecoff in a playoff. The weather was the problem. A deluge fell opening day. Many of the participants were of the opinion that a postponement was in order, but the USGA did not agree. Adjustments had to be made; the new longer tees had to be abandoned because they were so muddy they could not provide satisfactory footing. The wet conditions posed a problem for Gene for only two days. He shot 79 in each of the first two rounds, and missed the cut by eight shots. Two strokes behind Gene for those two rounds was a 17-year-old amateur named Jack Nicklaus who, like Gene before him, was making his U.S. Open debut at Inverness.

Gene was pretty worked up that the USGA had not postponed the opening round. He blamed television commitments as the reason the

USGA had forged ahead, and he asked this question: "Is this title golf or a tv show?"

Gene made his last appearance at a U.S. Open the following year at the Southern Hills Country Club in Tulsa, Oklahoma. He had qualified with ease, finishing fourth in a field of 138 players vying for seven spots at the Westchester Country Club. Weather was again a problem for the Open. Instead of rain, this time it was searing heat and high winds. The heat took its toll on 56-year-old Gene. The first day, he posted an 84 and on the second day an 80, leaving him 10 strokes from the cut line.

The year 1960 marked Gene's 40th year in professional golf and it got off to an impressive start, as he was awarded quite an honor. At that time the Cooperstown of golf was located in a five-story brownstone on 38th Street in the Murray Hill section of Manhattan that housed the USGA headquarters, Golf House. Early in January, a special ceremony took place honoring Gene's accomplishments in golf. A portrait in oils of Gene was unveiled, and would be displayed in a special area of Golf House. Gene's would be the sixth such portrait to be displayed. The other five were of Bobby Jones, Walter Hagen, Francis Ouimet, Glenna Collett Vare—considered the greatest female golfer America had produced to that point—and John Reed, who many considered the father of golf in America and one of the men who spearheaded the founding of the USGA.

In 1961, Gene got a crack at another job in television as the host of a new series, *Shell's Wonderful World of Golf*. The show featured a weekly head-to-head match-up between some of the biggest names in golf and occasionally a not-so-well known, at least in the United States. The matches were played across the globe at a wide range of courses from St. Andrews, the home of golf, to the Royal Selangor Golf Club in Kuala Lumpur, Malaysia, and the Ranelagh Golf Club in Buenos Aires, Argentina.

The series ran from 1962 to 1970. Matches were edited to fit the show's hour length. Gene, decked out in his knickers, was the host and through his performances on the show he soon became known as the game of golf's foremost ambassador. The show included a 10-minute travelogue on the host country that was credited with boosting tourism, especially among golfers who were interested in playing the courses featured on the show.

Midway through the show's run, the squabbles they had had 15 years before were put behind them, and Jimmy Demaret joined the show as

Gene's cohost. They were an ideal pairing that produced a wealth of entertaining banter. Some of their back-and-forth ended up on the editing room floor because it was out-of-bounds for 1960s television audiences.

In 1966, the show won an Emmy in the category of sports programming. This made Gene the second graduate of the Apawamis Golf Club caddie yard to win television's highest honor. The first had been Gene's caddie cohort, Ed Sullivan. His show, *Toast of the Town*, had debuted in 1948. It won the Emmy for best variety series in 1956. The following season, the show's name was changed to the *Ed Sullivan Show*.

In the spring of 1969, Gene said farewell to farm life when he sold the farm in Germantown and purchased a home in New London, New Hampshire. He and Mary would spend the late spring and summer there and most of the fall and winter in Marco Island on Florida's Gulf Coast, a locale they had fallen in love with in the 1960s.

In early October 1969, Gene and the rest of the golf world mourned the passing of Walter Hagen. Walter had for all practical purposes walked away from the game after the 1940 U.S. Open, an event he did not get to finish, and that was not by his own choosing. On day two, as had been his trademark for years, he showed up a few minutes late for his tee time. His group was about to play their second shots when he arrived. He hurriedly played his drive and caught up with his group and played the whole round. Upon its completion, he was advised by USGA officials that he was being disqualified for missing his tee time.

Hagen played socially until 1946 and then gave up the game, except for hitting an occasional shot on the front lawn of his home in Travers City, Michigan. In 1969 Walter succumbed to cancer, which he had been battling for the last two years.

A month after Walter's death, Gene was honored with an award at an event in New York City. Ed Sullivan was the master of ceremonies. The occasion was called the Americans of Italian Descent Salute at Madison Square Garden. Three other sports stars were honored for their achievements: Rocky Marciano, who retired as undefeated heavyweight champion after 49 bouts; NFL coaching legend Vince Lombardi; and the Yankee Clipper, Joe DiMaggio.

17

FINISHING AS A STARTER

Soon after the 1948 Masters, Bobby Jones was diagnosed with syringomyelia, a debilitating spinal disease that over the next 23 years would rob him of his mobility. He was soon required to use a cane, then a cane and a leg brace, then two leg braces and crutches, and finally a wheelchair. As the disease progressed, Bobby and Gene grew closer. During the years Gene was shooting *Shell's Wonderful World of Golf,* he corresponded often with Bobby, describing the locales and the various aspects of the courses on which the show's matches were being played.

When it reached the point when he was forced to use a wheelchair, Bobby would monitor the action during the Masters from his cabin along the 10th fairway. Gene always made it a point to go by the cabin after his round and go over with Bobby how he had played.

The last time Gene saw Bobby was after the 1971 Masters. He had propped himself into a standing position under the club's portico with the aid of a driver and waved farewell to Gene with a smile. Bobby passed away a week before Christmas that same year.

In 1973, Gene made what could be called an abbreviated farewell tour to major championship golf. He played in his last Masters. Of course, at the age of 71, making the cut was not in the cards. He shot 88 the first day. In his final competitive round in the tournament that he had played such a huge part in making an American sports classic, Gene, wearing a big smile as well as his signature knickers, shot an 86.

In July of that year, Gene was given one more opportunity to play in a major. The R&A, the association that Gene had often been critical of over the years, had offered him an exemption into the 1973 British Open, and Gene accepted.

The site of the Open Championship that year was Royal Troon, where in 1923 Gene had suffered one of the greatest disappointments of his career when he had a disastrous round on the final day of qualifying and failed to make the field. Whereas Gene's famous double eagle at Augusta had been witnessed by only a handful of people, he would make a shot at Troon that would be viewed by millions and millions around the world, thanks to television.

The eighth hole at Royal Troon is called the Postage Stamp. It measures 123 yards in length and is the shortest par-three in championship golf, but it rivals the 12th at Augusta in its dastardliness. Willie Park Jr., winner of the Open in 1889, is given credit for the Postage Stamp name. He reportedly described it as a pitching surface skimmed down to the size of a postage stamp. Its minuscule putting surface is difficult to hold, and anything less than a well-executed shot can run off the green and end up in one of the five deep bunkers that surround it.

The Postage Stamp has wreaked havoc on many of the biggest names in golf. In that 1923 Open Championship in which Gene failed to make the field, Walter Hagen made a double bogey there in the final round and finished second to Arthur Havers by one shot. In 1997 Tiger Woods was in contention in the final round until he reached the Postage Stamp; he took a six there and dropped off the leaderboard. In 1989, Greg Norman set a new course record of 64. His only bogey of the round came at the Postage Stamp.

At the Postage Stamp in his first round at the 1973 Open Championship, Gene teed up his ball and took a three-quarter swing with a 5-iron. His ball sailed high into the air as if he had used a more lofted club. It landed ten feet from the flag, took two bounces and then trickled up to the front of the cup and disappeared.

Cameras were rolling when Gene hit the shot, and in 24 hours it had been viewed around the world. One of the people who watched the shot on television was an old friend of Gene's whom he had not seen in over 40 years—Howard Hughes. Before Gene teed off for his second round the following day, he received a telegram from Hughes. After being seriously injured in a plane crash in 1946, Hughes, one of world's richest men, began retreating from the public eye. By the early 1960s he was as close as one could get to total seclusion. During much of that decade,

Hughes conducted all of his business while shuttered up on the top floor of the Desert Inn hotel in Las Vegas, and very few people ever laid eyes on him. Late in 1971, he slipped out of Las Vegas, and he and his entourage were now holed up on an entire floor of a hotel near Buckingham Palace in London. The press had the hotel staked out, hoping to get a photo or just a snippet of information about his activities. His telegram to Gene at least gave them something. They now knew that Hughes, who in his 20s had aspirations to be a championship golfer, still liked the game and that he watched television. His telegram to Gene read as follows:

> You have not changed a bit. You are as good as ever. Your accomplishment today refreshed many pleasant memories.
> Howard Hughes

On day two of the Open Championship, Gene had a much larger gallery following his play than he had the day before. As one might expect, there was quite a bit of interest as to what he might do for an encore at the Postage Stamp. But his tee shot was off line and ended up in a sand trap by the green. Those who stuck around to see him play his bunker shot were well rewarded, as the inventor of the sand wedge holed the shot from the bunker for a birdie two.

Although his second-round 81 matched with his opening 79 wasn't good enough to be around for the weekend, playing the Postage Stamp at three under par without ever using his putter has to be considered the gold standard for farewell performances.

In September 1974, Gene was named along with 12 other greats to the first class of the World Golf Hall of Fame, which had opened in Pinehurst, North Carolina, and has since moved to its current location near St. Augustine, Florida. The other 12 inductees were:

Patty Berg	Walter Hagen
Ben Hogan	Bobby Jones
Byron Nelson	Jack Nicklaus
Frances Ouimet	Arnold Palmer
Gary Player	Sam Snead
Harry Vardon	Babe Didrikson Zaharias

During his time in Pinehurst for the ceremony, Gene was asked by a reporter from the Associated Press to cite his biggest thrill in golf. Gene's answer was not what the reporter expected—it was not the epic shot at the 15th at Augusta. It was winning both the British Open and the U.S. Open in 1932.

Each year since 1935, the Masters had steadily grown in popularity, and so had the lore about Gene's double eagle. The fixation on that shot had begun and would continue to be a sore spot for Gene. He believed the allure of that one moment overshadowed all the other accomplishments he had made in the game.

In 1978, at a course owned by Jimmy Demaret in Austin, Texas, a golf tournament featuring legends of the game who had passed the half-century mark in age was held. The success of that event would soon spawn what has now become the Champions Tour. Players must wait until after their 50th birthday to participate. But once they achieve that milestone, the earnings potential is very sweet. In 2015, its three leading money winners—Bernhard Langer, Jeff Maggert, and Colin Montgomery—earned more than $2 million. The next 10 players on the list earned in excess of a million.

Fred Raphael, the producer of *Shell's Wonderful World of Golf*, was the driving force, along with Jimmy Demaret, for that first event in Austin. Its sponsor was Liberty Mutual Insurance. It was Gene who planted the seed for the event.

Back in 1963, the second season of *Shell's Wonderful World of Golf*, Gene and Fred were in Augusta for the Masters. Fred was spending some time with Gene after they had dined together. That evening, Gene called over to the Augusta National to obtain his tee time for that first round. When he hung up the phone he turned to Fred and said, "Tomorrow, 'the old legend Gene Sarazen is playing with the new legend Arnold Palmer.'"

In an interview with Dave Anderson of the *New York Times* about the long-term success of the Liberty Mutual Legends event and how it had fueled what would become the Champions Tour, Raphael recalled that phone call and said, "From the moment Gene Sarazen used the word legend that night, it stayed with me, and in 1978, we finally put it together."

Although he was no longer competing, Gene was diligent about making his annual pilgrimage to Augusta for the Masters. He enjoyed getting together with all the past winners at the Champions Dinner before the tournament, playing a few holes before the start of the tournament, and hanging around the clubhouse. He was always sought out by the press for an interview because he was still great copy.

In 1981, Gene became an official part of the next 18 Masters. In 1963, the tradition of having honorary starters at the Masters began. The initial roles were given to Gene's old rival and former British Open and PGA Championship winner, Jock Hutchison, and Fred McLeod, who had won the U.S. Open in 1908. They were both institutions at their respective home courses. Hutchison was the head professional at the Glen View Club outside of Chicago, where his tenure would span 35 years. McLeod was the head professional at the Columbia Country Club in Chevy Chase, Maryland, near Washington, DC. He took the position in 1912 and served the club until he retired in 1967, at which time the club made him pro emeritus and provided him with an apartment on the grounds.

Hutchison and McLeod would lead off the event on Thursday morning, and would play nine holes and sometimes a few more. Hutchison retired in 1973 due to declining health. McLeod carried on until the 1976 Masters. He died a month later and was buried on the grounds of the Columbia Country Club. Hutchison passed away in 1977 at the age of 93.

After McLeod died, there were no honorary starters until 1981, when Masters officials decided to revive the tradition and asked Gene and Byron Nelson to take on the roles. Having the man who had put the Masters on the map with his "shot heard 'round the world" in the opening ceremony added great panache to an event that was already overflowing with it.

A few years later, Sam Snead was also added as an honorary starter. As McLeod and Hutchison had done, the starters would hit the drives and then play nine holes. As the years progressed, it became a few holes and eventually, no holes at all, just the opening drive. No matter the length of their appearance, it was always a lump-in-throat moment.

Every year that has passed has added more clout to that shot back in 1935. There was a great deal of buzz about it on its golden anniversary in 1985, but Gene continued to grumble about how it overshadowed all the other aspects of his stellar career.

Since Gene's fateful shot in 1935, the 15th hole at Augusta has produced a mountain of drama on the final day, as those in contention play their second shots. In 1986, the cornerstone of Jack Nicklaus's extraordinary charge to his sixth and final Masters win was his second shot at 15.

His 4-iron from 202 yards almost went into the cup on the fly, producing the loudest roar from the gallery ever heard at Augusta. A few minutes later, Jack dropped a 12-foot putt for an eagle. Fifteen minutes later, Seve Ballesteros, who had the lead by one stroke, went for the green at 15 with his second shot. It splashed down in the pond.

On the way in, Jack followed up his eagle with birdies at 16 and 17 to win by one stroke over Greg Norman and Tom Kite. Seve's misfire at 15 led to a bogey. He also bogeyed 17 to finish in third, two strokes back.

One of the more interesting moments at the 15th hole came in1957. Doug Ford wanted to go for the green in two in his final round, but he almost had to fight with his caddie to do it. The day before, Ford was almost in the same location with his drive and had opted to go for the green in two. The shot carried the pond, but just barely. It struck the bank and rolled back into the water. He left the hole with a bogey six and at the end of the day was three strokes behind the leader.

When he reached the 15th in the final round, Ford had surged into the lead one stroke ahead of Sam Snead. His drive was very close to where it had reached in the third round, a distance of about 240 yards from the pin. Ford didn't hesitate—he was going for it again and reached over to his bag to pull out his 3-wood, but he met with resistance. His caddie, George "Fireball" Franklin, latched on to the club and wouldn't let Ford pull it from the bag. Fireball wanted him to lay up. They began tussling, much to the surprise and amusement of the gallery. Ford firmly told Fireball that Snead was right behind them and he for sure would not be laying up. Fireball gave up the club. The shot cleared the bank by an eyelash and held the green. Ford two-putted for birdie. He went on to win by three shots.

The big story at the conclusion of the 1993 Masters was what didn't happen at 15 in the last round. Chip Beck and Bernhard Langer were in the last pairing of the day. Langer was in the lead. Beck was three shots back. At 15, both had good drives that put them in position to go for the green. Standing in go-for-it range and three strokes behind, like Gene had been in 1935, everyone expected Beck to leave nothing in the bag and go for it. But Beck surprised everyone and decided to lay up. His third shot to the green was not a good effort, and he walked away with just a par. Meanwhile, Langer went for the green, made it with his second shot, and made a two-putt birdie, taking a four-stroke lead that would be the margin of victory. Beck parred in and hung on to second.

Beck took a wealth of criticism from the media and from golf fans. He had stood on the same hill where Gene had hit the most famous shot in golf history and sent the Masters on its way to greatness, but had not pulled the trigger.

Golfers are generally regarded as the most civil of all athletes. But even Langer piled on, telling Dave Anderson of the *New York Times*, "If I were in his shoes I would have gone for it if I had any chance." But Beck did get some rather surprising support. It was from the man who had been three shots down at the 15th hole in the final of a Masters and faced the same shot—Gene Sarazen.

For finishing second, Chip Beck received $183,600. Two strokes back, the four players who had tied for third took home $81,600. So by playing it safe, Beck had protected his big payday (by 1990s standards). Other than perhaps Ben Hogan, there has never been a golfing great who appreciated the value of a dollar more than Gene. In a post-tournament conversation with Beck, Gene brought up the fact that when he went for the green in 1935, second-place money was only $700 and that if he had been playing for the kind of second-place money they were paying out in the 1990s, he would have laid up, too.

Tiger Woods won the 1997 Masters, his first major championship, by 12 strokes at the age of 21. After Woods's win, Gene was asked what he thought of Tiger winning the Masters at such a young age. His terse reply was, "I won two majors when I was 20."

In 1999 Gene, 97 years old, made his final appearance at the opening ceremony at the Masters, clad in his knickers as always. He moved slowly and deliberately with a grin on his face. The grin changed into a broad smile when he slowly and deliberately delivered his driver to the back of the ball and he sent it 80 yards down the fairway.

Five weeks later, Gene passed away at a hospital in Naples, Florida. There was an outpouring of tributes and gracious comments about him. At his funeral service four days later on Marco Island, 800 were in attendance.

In planning his final arrangements, Gene had asked a man he had called out once in a well-publicized rant to deliver the eulogy—Ken Venturi. Where Gene had experienced an incredible high at Augusta with his epic shot, Venturi had experienced one of the all-time heartbreaking lows there in 1956. Playing as an amateur, he had held the lead for the first three rounds and started the final round with a four-stroke lead, only to shoot an 80 to lose by a stoke to Jack Burke Jr.

A few days after that horrible Sunday, it was reported that Venturi had blamed the pairings of the Masters tournament committee for his collapse. It had been the recent practice of the committee to put Byron Nelson with the leader in the last round. The two-time Masters champion had the personality, class, and demeanor that you would want in a playing partner.

Venturi asked the committee to make Nelson his playing partner. But the committee opted not to in this case because Nelson had been a close friend and mentor to Venturi for several years. Instead, Venturi was given Sam Snead as a partner, and they were anything but compatible. Venturi accused Sam of giving him the "freeze treatment."

Gene was contacted by Will Grimsley of the *Washington Post* at his farm back in Germantown for his comments on what Venturi had said. Gene called Venturi's comments "a crybaby's alibi" and that anyone who shot 80 in the final round of a golf tournament should be seen and not heard. He added that he had shot final rounds of 80 before, and had gotten away quickly and had gone into hiding. Gene cooled down at the end of his rant and said, "He has a great golf game and a wonderful competitive spirit. I think he is the most promising I've ever seen."

Ken Venturi would come close to winning the Masters several more times, and he would win the 1964 U.S. Open. He later became a golf analyst for CBS and was a fixture on the Masters telecasts for 35 years. Soon after that 1956 Masters, Gene and Ken developed a close personal relationship that grew stronger and stronger over the years. In the mid-1970s, Ken had joined Gene as a resident of Marco Island.

There was a twist of irony in Gene's passing. He died from complications of pneumonia, the same malady that had sent him away from a dusty factory floor environment and on to a career in golf some 80 years earlier.

BIBLIOGRAPHY

BOOKS

Barkow, Al. *Gettin' to the Dance Floor: An Oral History of American Golf.* New York: Atheneum, 1986.

Barkow, Al, and Mary Sarazen. *Gene Sarazen and Shell's Wonderful World of Golf.* Ann Arbor, MI: Clock Tower Press, 2003.

Bisher, Furman. *Furman Bisher: Face to Face.* Champaign, IL: Sports Publishing, 2005.

———. *The Masters and Augusta Revisited: An Intimate View.* Birmingham, AL: Oxmoor House, 1976.

Clayton, Ward. *Men on the Bag: The Caddies of Augusta National.* Ann Arbor, MI: Sports Media Group, 2004.

Darwin, Bernard, and Margret Hughes. *A Round with Darwin: A Collection of the Golf Writings of Bernard Darwin.* London: Souvenir Press, 1984.

Delery, John, and Angus G. Garber. *100 Years of the U.S. Open: A Century of Excellence.* New York: Metro Books, 2000.

Eubanks, Steve. *Augusta: Home of the Masters Tournament.* Nashville, TN: Rutledge Hill Press, 1997.

Feinstein, John. *The Majors: In Pursuit of Golf's Holy Grail.* New York: Little, Brown, 1999.

Flaherty, Tom. *The Masters: The Story of Golf's Greatest Tournament.* New York: Holt, Rinehart and Winston, 1961.

———. *The U.S. Open, 1895–1965: The Complete Story of the United States Championship of Golf.* New York: Dutton, 1966.

Fountain, Charles. *Sportswriter: The Life and Times of Grantland Rice.* New York: Oxford University Press, 1993.

Hagen, Walter, and Margaret Seaton Heaton. *The Walter Hagen Story.* New York: Simon & Schuster, 1956.

Hargreaves, Ernest, and J. M. Gregson. *Caddie in the Golden Age: My Years with Walter Hagen and Henry Cotton.* London: Partridge, 1993.

Jarman, Colin. *The Ryder Cup: The Definitive History of Playing Golf for Pride and Country.* Lincolnwood, IL: Contemporary Books, 1999.

Olman, John M. *The Squire: The Legendary Golfing Life of Gene Sarazen.* Cincinnati, OH: Olman Industries, 1987.

Owen, David. *The Making of the Modern Masters.* New York: Simon & Schuster, 1999.

Roberts, Clifford. *The Story of Augusta National Golf Club.* Garden City, NY: Doubleday, 1976.

Sampson, Curt. *The Masters: Golf, Money, and Power in Augusta, Georgia.* New York: Villard, 1999.

Sarazen, Gene, and Herbert Warren Wind. *Thirty Years of Championship Golf.* New York: Prentice-Hall, 1950.

Sommers, Robert. *The U.S. Open: Golf's Ultimate Challenge.* New York: Atheneum, 1987.

Sowell, David. *The Masters: A Hole-by-Hole History of America's Golf Classic.* Washington, DC: Potomac Books, 2007.

NEWSPAPERS

Atlanta Journal-Constitution
Augusta Chronicle
Boston Globe
Chicago Tribune
Los Angeles Times
Milwaukee Sentinel
New York Herald Tribune
New York Times
Pittsburgh Post-Gazette
St. Petersburg Times
The State (Columbia, SC)
Sydney Morning Herald
The Times
Washington Post

MAGAZINES

American Golfer
Golf
Golf Digest
New Yorker
Saturday Evening Post
Sports Illustrated
Time

ABOUT THE AUTHOR

David Sowell has written about golf and golf history for over two decades for numerous publications, including the United States Golf Association's *Golf Journal*. His 2003 book, *The Masters: A Hole-by-Hole History of America's Golf Classic*, was praised by *Library Journal* ("an entertaining read that enthusiasts will enjoy") and *Booklist* ("Sowell gives us the Masters in full flower"). He is also the author of *Ike, Golf, and Augusta*, published in 2012. He resides in Taylors, South Carolina.

9 781538 130964